Earth Energy

Betsey Lewis

Earth Energy
Return to Ancient Wisdom

Betsey Lewis

Earth Energy: Return to Ancient Wisdom
ISBN: 978-1491077580
Copyright © 2015 by Betsey Lewis

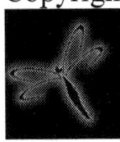

Dragonfly Dimensions Publishing
10400 W. Overland, #335
Boise, Idaho 83709-1449
www.dragonflydimensionspublishing.com
Library of Congress Cataloging in-Publication Data (Lewis, Betsey
— Spirituality—Environment—Native American—Ancient Wisdom

All rights reserved. No part of this book may be reproduced, scanned, photocopied, recorded or distributed in any printed or electronic form without written permission from the author.
Cover Photograph - Cliff Palace in Mesa Verde National Park by Betsey Lewis, Design by Dragonfly Dimensions Publishing (10.1)

DEDICATION

Dedicated to Mother Earth—our first Mother, who provides us with life-giving elements and abundant beauty through the Creator. For the Wisdom Keepers, the Grandmothers, Indigenous Elders and the Spiritual Leaders who have shown us the path back to natural living and the ancient ways of honoring our planet. May future generations acknowledge and honor the Oneness in all life and return to Ancient Earth Wisdom.

My heartfelt gratitude to my friend, spiritual leader of the Western Shoshone Nation, Corbin Harney, who was a warrior of light for our planet, and to my spiritual mentor, Oglala Sioux ceremonial leader, Ed McGaa "Eagle Man," for sharing his wisdom on the natural way of life for the Rainbow Tribe and future generations.

Betsey Lewis

CONTENTS

Introduction	7
In the Beginning	15
Water Element	21
Earth Element	53
Fire Element	87
Air Element	101
Plant Spirits	109
Animal Spirits	121
Mineral Spirits	131
Spirit	141
A Dying Planet	147
Saving Earth	163
Earth Wisdom	183
Epilogue	197
Living Earth Wisdom	205
Bibliography	207
About the Author	211

Earth Energy

ONE WATER, ONE AIR, ONE EARTH

The old people used to say that the trees, the rocks, the birds, and the animals used to talk. They had a voice, and today, as I realize it, they still have a voice. My people always say that you have to take care of them in order for you to continue on. If you don't, when they die off, you are going to die with them.

—Spiritual Leader of the Western Shoshone Nation Corbin Harney (1920-2007)

Our planet is our spaceship. It looks very fragile from here, and it's very easy to take it for granted when we're living on it, when it seems so big and so massive. But it's not. It's very small and very fragile. —NASA Astronaut Sandra Magnus in 2009

Introduction

Something transformational is taking place on Mother Earth, our unique blue planet tucked away on the outer edge of the Milky Way Galaxy. Extreme weather has become the norm, increased earthquakes in strange places not known for earthquakes, mysterious booms heard worldwide, increased volcanic activity, sink holes forming everywhere, birds and sea creatures dying in large numbers, and unexplained lights in the sky. These are some of the images I was shown in prophetic dreams at the age of seven. My dreams are now reality—the time of great Earth changes has arrived!

Indigenous people worldwide have foreseen the coming changes for many decades and tell us the changes will herald a new Earth. They tell us it is imperative that we return to the natural way of living as Earthkeepers, like they practiced and like their ancestors practiced eons ago. Once we do, our planet will return to balance—*ayni*. Although there are a great number of spiritual evolved people on the planet at this time, we haven't reached a total awakening. The indigenous people see a time we will be forced to awaken from our slumber and return to ancient wisdom by Earth changes.

The Hopi, the Inca and shaman speak of a purification time when Earth will turn or flip on its axis. Andrean prophecy tells of a coming period of transformation, when the Condor and the Eagle align, and a time of cosmic overturning of time and space that will signal the end of an era. This will be a time of humanity raising their consciousness and a new beginning. There will be a new relationship with Mother Earth and a Golden Age.

During this time of purification many will choose to leave, and those who do remain, will find new ways to live in harmony and gratitude with our Mother. The new children coming into the world now are old souls who are reincarnating very quickly, sensing they have an important role in the coming changes. These children bring a higher vibrational rate with them and enhanced psychic gifts—for they are the *new evolved human*.

This book is about honoring Mother Earth and all things on Earth. It's about returning to a simpler life, a more spiritual life, a more compassionate life, and a more caring life. By incorporating the lessons and knowledge, both ancient and indigenous inside this book, you will be on your way to creating a new future, and a new world. When we reconnect with the Living Library of Mother Earth, we connect to the mysteries, the age old secrets of spirit beings that watch and guide our planet. The shamans, the elders, the holy men and women practiced ceremonies for ages connecting to these benevolent beings that exist in the elements of our world. When we stop destroying the elements—Earth, Wind, Fire, Air, Water, and become balanced with these spirit beings, we'll discover that we can communicate with them. We will be aware of nature's signs and warnings.

Native teachings are based on Earth law and Nature herself. They teach us that everything is alive and has consciousness, even rocks, and all the elements are associated with dimensional beings like fairies, gnomes, angels. In our modern world, most of us have forgotten there is a transcendental world which is as real as the physical world, but we are so immersed in our material world we have forgotten the ethereal world. Also, as we destroy the elements, we are destroying ourselves.

The Lakota people have a phrase, *Mitakuye Oyasin,* which means, we are related to all things. The Lakota people, indigenous people and the ancient ones have always seen the interconnectedness of all life on Mother Earth. It is the oneness of prayer and respect for all forms of life: people, the four-legged animals, trees, rivers, finned creatures, winged creatures, rocks, mountains and valleys.

Ancient people understood Earth's uniqueness and how everything existed in perfect balance and how everything was connected in spirit. But today when we start harming, changing and destroying the elements through our egos, everything becomes unbalanced and chaotic. Ancient people knew the elements not only existed outside us but within us. We are ONE with the cosmos. In order to honor Mother Earth they practiced sacred ceremonies and called on the elements to guide them and protect them. Nothing was taken for granted.

Fast forward to present day and our planet suffers from unconscionable abuse and neglect. There are currently 7.2 billion humans living on Earth, and most of the billions of souls on Earth have forgotten their role as Earthkeepers and how exceptional and precious our planet really is in the Solar System. We now stand at a precipice where we can either take action and heal our planet or watch our oceans, lakes and rivers die, species vanish, and all our natural resources disappear. We are running out of time to repair the damage the collective "we" have unleashed on the planet in the last hundred years.

Maya Grandmother Flordemayo, one of the elders of the International Council of Thirteen Indigenous Grandmothers, said it best in *Grandmothers Counsel the World,* authored by Carol Schaefer, "To think that in a hundred years, we've lost total consciousness of everything. We humans have disrespected so much that in this time of movement, where the celestial doors have opened and heavenly beings are coming from the four directions to help us, but if we don't do what we've been asked to do, well...the results will be sad. We must learn how to wake up and stay awake during these dark and changing times."

Many of the worldwide environmental changes were foretold in native prophecy have already come to pass: the greenhouse effect, extreme changes in the seasons and in the weather, famine, disease, the disappearance of wildlife, and the hole in the ozone layer that native people refer to as "the hole in our lodging."

Another member of the Thirteen Indigenous Grandmothers, Grandmother Clara of the Amazon, spoke of her visit with the Star Beings. "Humanity and the Earth are being cleansed of the accumulated negativity caused by humanity's greater orientation to the material world and to technology, which has caused us to lose our connection to the Spirit World and to nature. We are destroying our planet and ourselves as a result of our materialism. Since nature is the source of our visions and centers us in Truth, the more we destroy nature, the less able we are to live in balance and wisdom and the more wars, disease, and disharmony we create."

I do not consider myself a shaman in any sense; I'm certainly not indigenous, nor do I have all the answers, but I do consider myself an Earthkeeper, and continue to do my best to heal our planet in ceremony and in prayer. I discovered the miracle of nature at an early age while growing up in rural southwestern Idaho. For me, nature was alive in everything—the rocks, the rivers, lakes, mountains, wind, weather, trees, and all creatures indigenous to Idaho and the Northwest. Mother Earth was my teacher and I was a student eager to learn about her. I'm not sure where this knowing came from, but it was always there from my earliest memories. Having parents, who loved the wilderness, camping, hunting, and mining, certainly enhanced my love of the environment.

Of course, at the time I was much too young to understand that everything on our planet has a consciousness, even rocks, but I sensed the importance of nature. A river, a pond, a lake, and the mighty ocean, all have their own distinct voice and spirit. And like humans, the elements have their own personalities and moods—a placid lake can transform into angry waves, the ocean can produce tsunami waves, and a river that once flowed quietly through a valley can become raging water destroying everything in its path.

During the 1950s, my parents spent summers in the Northern Nevada desert where my grandfather owned mining property. In this wildness area I observed deer, bobcats, jack rabbits, ground squirrels, and all kinds of birds. Years later my parents purchased Dierkes Lake, a mile-long spring-fed lake in the Snake River Canyon of Southern Idaho, formed by a collapsed lava tube. Originally the lake had been an apple orchard during the turn of the twentieth century until spring water began bubbling up from the ground and pouring into the valley basin. Ten years later a lake had formed, one mile long with of depth of one-hundred feet.

The lake was a magical place for my younger sister Kathy and me, where we lived in the water during the summer months—swimming, diving off rocks, water skiing and boating. We rode our horses, fished, hiked to the upper crater lakes and assisted our parents in the concession stand, collecting the entrance fee and selling soda and candy. Our animal family consisted of three Siamese cats, several dogs, three horses, chickens, and a few sheep. The Lake's wildlife consisted of porcupine, rock chucks, coyotes, birds, ducks, geese, rabbits, snakes, and an occasional swan.

My only escape from turbulent family life was hiking alone to an upper lake, swimming to a secluded part of the lake or sitting on a large granite boulder listening to the birds and watching the clouds pass by. Water was cathartic for me. Whenever I sought my private world of nature, I spoke to nature and to God—because I could see God's creation in everything. I soon learned water had a consciousness and a personality. On some days the lake was still and reflective as a mirror, but then a storm could quickly transform the water into angry white caps. Growing up in this wondrous environment taught me that everything is alive and full of energy.

Today, I never imagined Earth's natural resources would be destroyed at such an alarming rate as it has in the last fifty plus years. What will future generations see and experience on Mother Earth? Certainly not the beautiful Earth I experienced during the fifties and sixties. The utter lack of regard for Mother Earth and her creatures always brings me to tears.

We are seeing more Earth changes and as we enter a window of increased activity, it's imperative that we trust our intuition, the animals and Mother Earth to warn us. When we learn to trust Mother Earth and her warnings, we are using Earth Wisdom practiced by ancient people and indigenous people globally.

Mother Earth showed her fierceness on December 26, 2004 from an undersea megathrust earthquake and subsequent tsunami off the coast of Sumatra, Indonesia that resulted in the deaths of 230,000 people in fourteen countries. The Native people in the outer islands understood nature and sensed this event before it happened. They managed not to suffer any fatalities like the mainlander people suffered. Even wild and domestic animals seemed to sense what was about to happen and fled to safety. According to eye witnesses elephants screamed and ran for higher ground, dogs refused to go outdoors, flamingos abandoned their low-lying breeding areas and zoo animals rushed into their shelters and could not be enticed to come back out.

The next major disaster took place on April 20, 2010 following the explosion and sinking of BP's Deepwater Horizon oil rig that took eleven lives. Oil began gush from the site into the Gulf of Mexico. It is estimated 4.9 million barrels of oil flowed into the Gulf for 87 days. Subsequent attempts to harness the oil with a toxic dispersants failed, and resulted in the death of thousands of fish, shrimp and other sea creatures, and the deaths of countless birds and wildlife. Today, it is reported the oil continues to flow into the ocean.

The big oil companies still haven't learned their lesson from the largest accidental marine oil spill in the history of the petroleum industry. Deep water oil drilling continues worldwide, endangering wildlife, ocean life and human life.

Another catastrophic Earth event occurred on Friday, March 11, 2011 when Japan experienced a 9.0 megathrust earthquake that lasted six minutes, followed by a powerful tsunami that reached heights of up to 40.5 meters (133 ft.) in Miyako and which, in the Sendai area, travelled up to 10 km (6 mi.) inland. The earthquake moved Honshu (the main island of Japan) 2.4 m (8 ft.) east and shifted the Earth on its axis by estimates of between 10 cm (4 in.) and 25 cm (10 in.). An estimated 20,000 people died that day.

Fukushima Daiichi nuclear disaster resulted when the plant was hit by a tsunami when a meltdown occurred in three of the plant's six nuclear reactors. The rate at which contaminated water has been estimated at 300 tons a day a few months after the disaster, and there are conflicting reports of the current flow.

Humanities foolishness for Mother Earth rages on, and now fracking may be to blame for hundreds of swarm earthquakes hitting central Oklahoma, Kansas, Arizona, New Mexico, Texas and southeastern Oregon, places not known for earthquake activity.

As our planet experiences catastrophic weather, droughts, wildfires, powerful earthquakes, tsunamis, disastrous floods, catastrophic hurricanes like Katrina in New Orleans (2005) and Sandy (2012), and devastating tornadoes, we should understand that Mother Earth won't allow our abuse and disregard any longer. She wants to survive despite our destructive ways and she is fighting back. Clearly something inexplicable is happening to our planet.

The ominous booms that thunder across the sky, some call "skyquakes" are erupting all over the planet. People are becoming fearful of what the bizarre hums, explosive booms, howls, and moans might represent. Some have even described a horn sound and have suggested Angel Gabriel blowing his horn to announce

Armageddon.

From Russia to Australia, from Chile to the Eastern Coast of the United States, people are reporting these sounds. People are asking if these are warnings of a catastrophic Earth event approaching. These harmonics may signal a massive Earth core slippage or as some believe the total shift of the Earth's poles. Speculation is Earth's liquid core is spinning at a different rate than the planet's rotation and the slippage is causing the migration of the Earth's magnetic field.

Although some conspiracy theorists suggest skyquakes are a product of the military's top-secret High Frequency Active Auroral Research Program (HAARP) located in Gakona, Alaska, others believe the harmonics are from deep within the Earth traveling from a mutating core through the layers of the planet to the surface. The sky acts as a sounding board capturing and magnifying the sonic and electric frequencies shot from the center of Earth. The flashes of light are a product of piezoelectricity, created when rocks deep within the Earth begin to grind together under extreme stress.

Earth hasn't always been a peaceful place. Millions of years ago Earth was consumed in transformation where seas suddenly rose, islands disappeared, continents moved and flooded, volcanoes unleashed their furry, and mighty mountain ranges like the Andes and Himalayas rocketed from the depths of the ocean reaching many thousands of feet in the air within a matter of hours. Much of the United States was once covered in water and ancient seas. Today fossils and seashells can be found from North America to South America's jagged mountain peaks.

Rocks with Earth's crust contain crystals. It is known that prior to an earthquake the stored strain of energy is released as the fault slips and rocks return to their unstrained state and "earthquake lights" are produced. This appears to be happening everywhere but without the earthquakes. Slipping strata with the bowels of the planet create incredible pressures so great that temperatures soar and metals flow like liquids. Water in the Earth becomes superheated plasma and interacts with layers of quartz crystals emitting harmonics audible as a hum, boom, or moan creating Earth lights and skyquakes echoing across the sky. Earthquake lights were reported in the sky before the Fukushima earthquake in Japan in 2011, the 1971 Southern California earthquake and as far back as the 1906 San Francisco earthquake.

Instead of fearing Mother Earth's changes, if we reconnect to her, we will understand the signs and warnings when she is about to move our world in a big way. That's how ancient ingenious people survived for thousands of years; by trusting their innate sixth sense—that forewarned them of earthquakes, storms, floods, warring tribes and fierce animals.

We can no longer ignore Mother Earth's warnings. Prophecies speak of the cleansing that will take place by volcanoes, floods, famines, disease, disappearance of wildlife, the greenhouse effect, and changes in the seasons. This book was written so that we—humanity will return to ancient wisdom and become Earthkeepers, Wisdomkeepers and Rainbow Warriors again—that we will return to the natural way of Earth living—respecting and honoring everything. That we will understand the signs in the sky, the water, and in the creatures of Earth when our planet begins to move us. It is in this mindfulness that we emerge into Mother Earth and become One with Life.

Indigenous people believe that what we do today, at this moment, will affect the next seven generations, and so it is our responsibility to teach the children these sacred lessons about Mother Earth's Living Library, so they will continue the healing lineage of the Ancient Ones that came before us. When humans no longer feel they are superior above all life, when the human ego is no longer in command, then peace, balance and harmony will reign on Earth.

I've written *Earth Energy* from the knowledge I've gained from nature, my visions and my indigenous teachers, to offer hope, not fear, where the essence of respect, love, and pure heart manifests in all humans and is practiced daily. When we awaken to our relationship to the cosmos and Earth Wisdom, life will return to *ayni—balance.*

CHAPTER ONE
In the Beginning

Aboriginal leader Alinta aka Lorraine Mafi Williams 1940-2001

For thousands of years Australian Aboriginals have lived in harmony with Mother Earth, but there was a time long before they arrived on Earth, they came from a far distant place in the stars, according to their ancient legends. In Steven McFadden's book, *Ancient Voices, Current Affairs: The Legend of The Rainbow Warriors*, he cited the late Australian Aboriginal leader, visionary, activist and filmmaker, Alinta aka Lorraine Mafi Williams, and her wise words to the world.

TIME TO TELL EVERYONE
We, the Australian Aboriginals, have been on our traditional land, the Land of the Everlasting Spirit, for tens of thousands of years. Our culture is rivaled by no other, though we have been in seclusion for the last two hundred years. We are re-emerging from that seclusion now to show ourselves as no one has ever seen us.

Our creation stories take us back into Dreamtime, beginning when the Earth was one land mass. At that time the four races—red, yellow, black, and white, lived side by side. There, they lived as one people, creating a world of harmony, balance and mystery.

As Aboriginals we have kept our culture intact for thousands of years into the present time. Now we are ready to share our wondrous culture with the other people of the world. That is my work through my teaching and my films.

It took the white people only fifty years to destroy a million years of our culture, but the core of it still remains strong. We haven't forgotten. Our elders are telling us to go out and tell everyone, so that no one can say they didn't hear.

LAND OF THE EVERLASTING SPIRIT

Whenever our elders or shaman people—all our elders are shaman people—talk about our history and our beginning, our creation, they always talk about the time when the Earth was one land mass. They speak of time before the cataclysm came that split the Earth up into the continents.

This is our story, our mythology. Our land, Australia is called Arunta, the Land of the Everlasting Spirit. Our old people tell us that we originally came from a planet that had seen its time and just blew up.

See, our people were like refugees, and they went and lived in the stars in the Milky Way. Then seven spirit brothers and seven spirit sisters came to Earth. They came when the Earth was one big land mass.

They came to erect an energy grid. Because, you see, the planet Earth is among the smallest of planets. And it is really not in the galactic system where all the other planets exist. We believe Earth is just a little bit outside the plane of the Milky Way galaxy in space. Because the Earth is so small, when the planets line up in a certain way, the pull of the galactic energy is so strong that it could just suck planet Earth into the spiral plane of the galactic system and toss it all around.

So, my people were given the knowledge to create this energy grid because the planet that they were previously on did not have such a protective structure, and it was destroyed. They realized that their new home, Earth, needed to have such an energy grid in a strong, healthy condition to withstand periodic energy pulsations from the galaxy.

Otherwise, it would quickly be drawn into the plane of the galaxy and experience devastating turbulence.

But my ancestors had learned this lesson, and so they came to Earth to erect an energy grid, or an Earth truss, to help the Earth when it undergoes its changes.

(Lorraine referred to the ley lines that encircle Earth.)

THE SACRED RAINBOW SERPENT

In our old way we call the energy grid Boamie, the Sacred Rainbow Serpent, whose colors reflect the beauty of the Earth and sky, the Rainbows. The multicolored coils of the Rainbow Serpent are reflected in the precious stones that are concealed in the Earth's crust. It is called the Rainbow Serpent because it has all the colors of the rainbow, gold and silver, of course, and the diamonds, the rubies, the emeralds, and the uranium. You see, it is the foundation, the Earth's crust. They are the particular substances that keep the energy grid strong and the Earth solid when the planets line up every so often and threaten to draw the Earth into the galactic energy swirl.

Since my people erected the energy grid, the Earth just sort of sails through the periodic planetary lineups without any difficulties. So that's my people's responsibility. Both men and women are very knowledgeable in how the energy grid works for the whole system. We know what each mineral in the Earth is supposed to do, and what men's and women's responsibilities are to keep the grid strong and healthy.

THE BALANCE IS IN JEOPARDY

We are very concerned about the energy grids of the Earth. They are there to help the Earth maintain its balance. Crystals and other minerals feed energy to the energy grid. They have been used for millions of years that way. For the health of the Earth, the crystals must be free to let energy flow to the grid.

But now minerals, metals and jewels have been removed from the Earth to such an extent that the balance is in jeopardy. Uranium, in particular, is important for this task. When it is all gone, the Earth will be right out of balance.

The mining has an influence on the human race, too, and the human body. The human being is a link between the Heavens and the Earth. By keeping our bodies in balance and in harmony, we can keep the Earth healthy, and that in turn supports our health. You see, it's a cycle. I used crystals in healing, but I do not believe they should be taken from the Earth to be used as ornaments. It's more valuable to leave them in the Earth. The same applies with uranium.

AT A CRUCIAL JUNCTURE

We have been told that within every one million years, there is a seven-thousand- year-long Earth shift. Then we begin to go into a new world, like we are doing now. By our reckoning, we are actually at the end of a seven-thousand-year shift now and we are beginning to enter a new million-year-long epoch.

Our people and our teachings are very similar to the teachings of the North American Indians. But we have different interpretations and we know our responsibility—taking care of the Earth through the energy grids. We perform our task by giving thanks to the Earth through the songs, dances and ceremonies.

Right now there are two things. The Earth is undergoing its earthly changes, which is normal for this time in our development. But because there's been so much destruction to the energy grid, especially the gold, which is nearly exhausted already—and now they are after the uranium—there is great danger to the stability of the Earth.

Gold has driven men mad for thousands of years, leading them to lie, steal, cheat, murder, and make war...all this wickedness to get the gold. Humanity has become greedy and as a result, wicked. That has led to fighting, war, and disease. People have forgotten their responsibility to the Earth, for want of the gold. And now it's the uranium.

As well as the Earth, humanity has to go through its changes. We've all got to rejuvenate and to create a new world on the same physical substance. And we are going through it. There's no safe place on Earth. We've just got to ride it out, but if we are in balance within ourselves and in balance with the Earth, then we are healthy.

At the end of each change—every time we come into a new

world—the Great Creator says: 'OK humanity, you must start your change now, too, and go into the new world—but you must do it in accordance with the Earth, as well as yourself, with heart.

It's interesting that besides the Australian Aboriginals the Maya of Mesoamerica speak of a time when they came from the stars.

When I went to the coast, the ocean water there looked sad to me. The water is saying, "I need help." Water talks like we do. It breaths air like we do. It's hard to believe, but it does. Everything drinks water, and everything's got a life to it. —Spiritual Leader of the Western Shoshone Nation Corbin Harney

CHAPTER TWO
Water Element

Water – female, Color blue, Direction- West and season – autumn

Of all the planets in our Solar System, Earth stands out as the only unique "blue planet." When viewed from outer space, Earth is a vivid blue marble, where water covers 70.9 percent of our planet's surface. No other planet in the entire solar system has an ocean and ecology like Earth.

Less than 5 percent of that water is fresh, and much of it is locked up in ice sheets or deep within the ground. Today, our oceans, rivers, lakes, and streams are polluted by sewage, industrial waste, pesticides, oil, and radiation from the Fukushima nuclear plant in Japan.

When I was growing up the thought of paying for a bottle of pure drinking water would have been a ludicrous thought, yet here we are in the twenty-first century drinking purified water from plastic bottles. With well-over 7.2 billion humans on the planet, and growing, our natural resources are vanishing at an unprecedented rate. At the rate that we are consuming water plus the severe drought affecting many areas of the world, we have a perfect storm for global water wars.

Historian David Soll wrote in his book, *Empire Water*, "Clean water is no longer a free gift of nature. It is a shared resource that can be preserved only through judicious investments and active engagement." Water is a living entity with a consciousness. We can no longer look at water in the same over-abundant way and think it will flourish from our neglect. We must view it as a sacred living, breathing entity like our ancestors did or it will perish, and so will we.

Water is an amazing substance that can transform into many forms; ice, steam, snow and in the fluid state. Water is the most life sustaining gift of Mother Earth, her life-blood. Without water most living inhabitants on this planet would not exist. Water flows outside us and with within us, and it cleanses and it heals everything. Life grows from it and flourishes.

The element of water teaches us that it has great power to cut down the tallest mountains and create the deepest canyons and should be respected for its immense strength. Archaeologists have recently discovered ancient cities that vanished beneath the oceans thousands of years ago, destroyed by a deluge of water.

Water can be soft, cold, hot, and healing but always transmutable and ever-changing like human emotions. Water teaches us to be flexible and gentle, fierce and powerful and at the end of our life journey we too flow into the great ocean of unknown. Water shapes the land with rivers, lakes, glaciers, mountains, and canyons. Water is the home of countless organisms that contribute to the life cycle of planet Earth. It is one giant symbiotic organism.

New research at the Aerospace Institute of the University of Stuttgart in Germany supports the theory that water has memory. Experiments revealed that each droplet of water from the same source has a different face. Each totally unique. They wondered if water has an "imprint" of energies to which it had been exposed. The theory was first proposed by the late French immunologist Dr. Jacques Benveniste in a controversial article published in 1988 in

Nature as a way of explaining how homeopathy works.

If Benveniste is right, just think what that might mean to the world. More than 70 percent of our planet is covered in water and the human body is made up of 60 percent water; the brain, 70 percent; the lungs, nearly 90 percent. Our energies might be traveling out of our brains and bodies and into those of other living beings of all kinds through imprints on this magical substance. Think of how rivers and lakes carry an infinitesimal amount of information and data, and when we drink from it, we are infused with the information at a cellular level. So oceans and rivers and rains might be transporting all manner of information throughout the world—both positive and negative.

The First Nations peoples of North America have a special relationship with water, built on their subsistence ways of life that extends back thousands of years. Their traditional activities depend on water for transportation, for drinking, cleaning, purification, and provides habitat for the plants and animals they gather as medicines and foods. Their ability to access good water shapes these traditional activities and their relationships with their surroundings. As Indigenous peoples, First Nations recognized the sacredness of their water, the interconnectedness of all life and the importance of protecting their water from pollution, drought and waste.

Water is the giver of all life and without clean water all life on Earth would perish.

Indigenous people throughout the world have always claimed a special relationship with nature. Many shaman and medicine men have called upon the water spirits to bring rain to drought areas. Remarkably their prayers and ceremonies are heard and rain is produced. It is said the term "Rain Dance" came into being during the days of Native American relocation by the U.S. government who banned certain religious ceremonies like the Ghost Dance or Sun Dance. The tribes in suppressed areas were forbidden to perform the Sun Dance, so they called it their "Rain Dance." Today the rain dance has been passed down through oral tradition, and many American Indians keep these rituals alive today.

Aboriginal people in the traditional communities of the far north of the Northern Territory of Australia still practice their ancient ceremonies and rituals. These remain of crucial importance to their lives and involve the whole community. Often these ceremonies are strongly associated with death, or, more precisely, for the souls of people who have departed from this life and joined the "Dreaming," the timeless continuum of past, present and future. Sacred Dreaming is where mythological ancestral beings travelled and caused the natural features of the country to come into being by their actions.

In Numbulwar, an aboriginal tribe on the eastern shore of the Gulf of Carpentaria has a ceremony called "Ngarrag." Actors begin first and then the Yirritja men are painted with designs representing their "Dreaming" or clan association. There are many different rituals, some taking place on secret ceremonial ground, where they assume the spirit beings of the planet. The ceremony ends in the ritual of bathing where the entire clan goes to the beach and immerses themselves, dancing in the sea and washing off the ochre and clay that was painted on them earlier in the ceremony. Dreamtime beings of the mythical past leave them in their songs and painted designs on their bodies behind and re-emerge from the water as people again.

We've seen the power of water with Mother Nature at her worst in tsunamis, torrential rains, floods, avalanches and natural geysers. In all of water's fierceness, it has a healing side. It can be harnessed to supply electricity to our homes, it supplies water to our deserts and makes it possible to plant crops, and gives life to countless species on the planet including water beings—humans. Without water our world would look like Mars, desert-like and devoid of life.

Water creates our weather. Water evaporates as vapor from oceans, lakes, and rivers; is transpired from plants; condenses in the air and falls as precipitation; and then moves over and through the ground into water bodies, where the cycle begins again. Mother Nature is a perfect organism.

Moving water found in ocean waves, waterfalls, rivers, release negative charged ions in the atmosphere. Negative and positive ions refer to electrical charge plus or minus. Negative electrical charges have good effects on humans, while positive-charged ions have bad effects on our health.

The word ion is derived from the Greek word meaning, "to go" or "to move." An ion is an atom or molecule in which the total number of electrons is not equal to the total number of protons, giving the atom a net positive or negative electrical charge. Ions can be produced in nature and by chemical means. An atom is electrically neutral when the number of electrons surrounding the nucleus (or nuclei) is equal to the atomic number. It becomes a positive ion if one of more electrons is missing or it becomes a negative ion if it has one more extra electron.

For eons prophets, sages and wisdomkeepers have sought higher spiritual experiences and consciousness on mountains or near waterfalls or near oceans. This is no accident—negative ions can be found in the air near waterfalls, mountains, beaches and forests. These are among those places where ionization levels are the highest and in complete and natural balance.

The Greek physician Hippocrates noted 2,300 years ago that his patients benefited from taking long walks near the sea or in the mountains. Even baptism in "living water" marks the beginning of Christianity as written in the Bible when John the Baptist was baptized by Jesus in the Jordan River.

Jesus was said to have harnessed stormy seas by calming it and walking upon it. The miracle described how Jesus sent his disciples by ship to the other side of the Sea of Galilee while he remained behind to pray. As night fell a windstorm created huge waves for the ship. In the midst of the storm the disciples saw Jesus walking on the sea toward them. Frightened, they thought they were seeing a spirit when Jesus told them not to be afraid. Jesus then entered the ship and calmed the storm, and they arrived safely on shore. According to a detailed account found only in Matthew, Peter had the ability to "walk on water," but he became afraid and began to sink, but Jesus rescued him. Was this a literal story or one that was used to teach a lesson of faith? Perhaps both.

It is believed that Michel de Nostre-Dame—Nostradamus, an astrologer and a physician from the sixteenth century, used water and astrology to divine the past, present and future. It is believed he used a bowl of water to see into the future. He used a tripod to hold the bowl then touched the tripod with the wand, dipped the wand in the water and then touched the hem of his robe. He then looked deep into the water and viewed the future. Many believed that Nostradamus actually used a form of self-hypnosis or meditation. Some followers of Nostradamus even believe he foretold events into the twentieth and twenty-first centuries that included predictions of Hitler, World War I and II, and even John F. Kennedy's assassination written in his 1555 book, *The Centuries*.

Was Nostradamus actually remote viewing by concentrating into the bowl of water? Perhaps he understood the power of water to project an image of the future when one meditates on a question. The most common media of scrying or viewing the future was with a reflective, translucent or luminescent substance such as crystals, stones, glass, mirrors, water, fire, or smoke.

Waterfalls have the highest concentration of negative ions, but negative ions can be found in mountains, rapid moving water such as rivers and oceans, and in dense vegetation such as forests or rain forests.

While living in Los Angeles, California for twenty-five years, I made an interesting observation during dry, hot Santa Ana winds and its effect on people. They'd become irritable and ill-tempered. The dry wind creates positive ions that can cause people to experience headaches, depression and an inability to concentrate. Similar winds in the United States known as Chinooks created the same phenomena in humans. In other places around the world, the dry winds are known as Sirocco, Zonda, Khamsin, and Mistral. In France during the Mistral winds more crimes are committed similar to the full moon phenomena.

Have you noticed how you feel before a major electrical storm where positive ions dance around the sky and ground? The ions in a cloud behave in the same way as the ions in a waterfall. The kinetic energy in the turbulent air strips off the electrons, leaving positive-charged ions. These free electrons are picked up by other atoms and molecules to create the negative-charged ions. The clouds are negatively charged and the Earth's surface becomes positively charged creating lightning. So if you feel irritable and out of sorts, blame those positive-charged ions.

Lightning ionizes the air, providing more free ions after the lightning strikes. American Indians have reported many cases of visions connected during thunder and lightning storms. I've also discovered that during electrical storms I experience increased psychic abilities and increased energy. Is it any wonder that indigenous people, shamans, and holy people, throughout the world understood the significance of ions and sought the mountains, waterfalls, oceans and forests for visions, spiritual enlightenment and clarity of thought?

Once the storm is underway and rain begins to fall, you will feel much better, even restful and at peace from the negative-charged ions.

In Jerusalem, researchers discovered that some people have sensitivity to barometric pressure. Their levels of serotonin in the brain increased just before and during desert wind conditions due to the positive ions. However, the serotonin dropped when these people were placed in negative-ionized rooms. Research conducted in France, Germany, Italy, and especially Russia found significant health benefits of health spas if they were situated near waterfalls. In Russia, such places are called "electrical resorts." In Japan waterfalls are considered powerful *kami*, where divine spirits reside.

Japanese author and entrepreneur Dr. Masura Emoto was an internationally-renowned researcher who gained worldwide acclaim by demonstrating how water is deeply connected to our individual and collective consciousness.

Emoto's ideas first appeared in the popular documentary, *What the Bleep Do We Know!?*. Although Emoto's work was widely considered pseudoscience that directly violates basic physics, his remarkable photographs of ice crystals proved something else was at work. His photographic work of water crystals published in his book *Message from Water, Vol. I, II and III*, sold over one-million copies internationally in twenty-two languages as well as his book *The Hidden Messages in Water* that sold over 500,000 in print copies.

Through the 1990's, Dr. Emoto performed a series of experiments observing the physical effect of words, prayers, music and environment on the crystalline structure of water. Emoto hired photographers to take pictures of water after being exposed to the different variables including frozen water so that they would form crystalline structures. The results were nothing short of extraordinary.

The experiments possibly proved that our thoughts have a major impact on our environment. That concept is relatively easy to grasp, but this extremely tangible evidence proved amazing. If our words and thoughts have this effect on water crystals, just think what consciousness *en masse* could produce? Our thoughts coalesce into solid matter, and as Dr. Emoto discovered, human thought can transform water molecules.

Eventually Emoto formed his non-profit organization, "International Water for Life," through which he dedicated his water research to achieving world peace.

There are incredible dynamics taking place in our oceans that began approximately 4.54 billion years ago. Scientists don't know how Earth arrived to be a water planet. Mars does contain polar ice and Jupiter's moon Ganymede is composed of approximately equal amounts of silicate rock and water ice, but nothing like Planet Earth. The most popular theory for Earth's water is that shortly after Earth formed, millions of asteroids and comets, saturated in water, slammed into our planet, releasing their water to form oceans, which sounds a bit preposterous to me. Still there is much mystery about the formation of our planet's oceans, lakes and rivers.

All living things on Earth require water. Humans are made up of 60 percent water. Animals and humans need water as a solvent for the nutrients and minerals needed by their cells. Plants rely on water too for the process known as transpiration. After being collected from the ground by their root system, water rises in the inner tubes to the rest of the plant or tree. All life on Earth evolved from the primordial seas where evolution magically created countless multi-level life forms—maybe and maybe not, if you believe in evolution.

Ley Lines

Ley Lines are invisible alignment and energy points said to be connected beneath sacred sites like churches, temples, stone circles, megaliths, holy wells, burial sites and other spiritual or magical places of importance. Their existence was first suggested in 1921 by amateur archaeologist Alfred Watkins, whose book, *The Old Straight Track,* brought the alignments to the attention of the wider public.

The extent of invisible or visible lines and harmonies connecting ancient sites and cities has always focused on their connection with areas of increased Earth energy and perhaps underground water. It is thought that the lines facilitated some aspect of ancient life so that cities and sites built along the same lines shared some mutual benefit. But what was that benefit? Here again there are many theories but nothing concrete.

Some theorists believe ley lines can be explained by the String Theory. This is a relatively new mathematical concept that allows for the existence of extra dimensions, including the passage from one dimension to another. String theory is a mathematical theory that tries to explain certain phenomena which is not currently explainable under the standard model of quantum physics. At its core, string theory uses a model of one-dimensional strings place of the particles of quantum physics.

String theory was initially developed in the 1970s in an attempt to explain some inconsistencies with the energy behavior of hadrons and other fundamental particles of physics.

Today New Age followers believe that there are certain sites on the Earth which are filled with special "energy." Stonehenge, Mt. Everest, Ayers Rock in Australia, Nazca in Peru, Sedona, Arizona, the Great Pyramid at Giza, Mt. Shasta, California, and Mutiny Bay, among other places, are believed to be places of special energy.

In his book, *Signs of the Gods,* best-selling author Erich Von Däniken mentioned the existence of an intricate network of ancient Greek sites, connected not just through straight alignment, but also in the relationship of the ratio of their distances to one another involving the famous Golden Section.

Däniken stated, "So how can we explain the mathematical perfectionism? How can we reconcile it with the standard of mathematical knowledge we attribute to prehistoric peoples? How did they know at what precise point they had to build? As the complicated relationships are only recognizable from a great height we must ask whether 'someone' worked out a geometrical network of sites all over Hellas, sticking flags in the ground saying: This is where you must build a temple"

It should be noted that a high number of UFO sightings have been seen over ley line areas and other sacred areas.

Changing Perceptions

Growing up in Idaho and then moving to Los Angeles during the late sixties, I believed somewhere I'd find the answer to mystical truths of life. This included my search for religious truths and so I attended different churches and religions that included Buddhism, African American Spiritualism, Judaism, New Age beliefs and several East Indian religions.

By the 1990s, I was drawn to American Indian spirituality and began attending Indian pow-wows, sweat lodge ceremonies and a couple of Vision Quests throughout the Western United States and the Northwest—Idaho, Oregon, Southern California and Calgary, Canada. It was in 1995 that I met two amazing Native American spiritual leaders; Corbin Harney of the Western Shoshone Nation and Ed McGaa "Eagle Man", Oglala Sioux Ceremonial Leader.

I first met Corbin in Boise, Idaho during a ceremony he conducted before a large group of people gathered one morning on a hill overlooking the City of Trees. Later that year, we began to organize a sacred Native American ceremony at actor Robert Redford's Sundance Resort in the Wasatch Mountains of Northern Utah. At first Mr. Redford was excited about having a Native American ceremony at his resort with Corbin Harney, but he indicated that if filming the *The Horse Whisperer* started during that time we had scheduled he wouldn't be available. That fall the movie began and Redford's assistant apologized that Mr. Redford was committed to his new movie, so our ceremony that Corbin and I had worked so hard on wouldn't take place. Through the years Corbin and I spoke many times, and I sensed a great sadness in his voice whenever we discussed the Earth and the horrible things taking place to the environment. He always mentioned Robert Redford and his disappointment that he was unable to meet his favorite actor. As the years went by Corbin's health declined and he didn't travel as much. We were never able to see each other again, and that saddened me greatly. Corbin was a powerful medicine man, a great teacher, who spoke from the heart about his concern for Mother Earth. He was also a courageous spiritual warrior who spoke out against the U.S. government's underground nuclear testing in Nevada and brought many people together to protest against it. Although Corbin went on to the Great Spirit in the sky on July 10, 2007, his words of wisdom will live on for future generations.

In Corbin's book, *The Way It Is: One Water, One Air, One Mother Earth,* he said, "There's a vision I've had from way back. Well, I've had visions about a lot of different things, but for instance, not too long ago, something came to me and talked to me about the water here. One time, when we were having a spiritual gathering when I was praying for the water, the water said to me, 'I'm going to look like water, but pretty soon nobody's going to use me.' The Creator, or the Spirit told me this, and I passed it on to the people who were there at the time. Now, wherever I go, the people talk about their water being contaminated, and they can't use it." Corbin was shown Earth's waters becoming toxic.

In another vision he was shown something at the Test Site in southern Nevada where they were drilling holes into the Earth and where they had blasted holes or set off bombs underground. The holes were filling with water. He saw the water being contaminated deep within the Earth where fresh water aquifers exist and deep springs. He said "My belief is to take care of what we've got in order to continue on. The Shoshone—well, not only the Shoshone, but the Native people of all the land, all over the world—believe in taking care of what's now here, in taking care of the world.

"Our Indian belief is, we are Natives of the land, and so we have to be with it. But nowadays we haven't been doing what we've been told to do, to be with the land. We have to take care of the living things here, all the plants, all the animal life. When we take the life of an animal, we have to tell it why we're taking its life. It has to know the reason. Then we give the animal a blessing and then we also give something back of whatever we're taking.

"We can't just go out and harvest whatever we want to. We have to talk to each living thing and bless it and say the reason why we're taking its life—the plant, the animal, the bird life, whatever. If they were to take our life, we'd want to understand why they were taking it. These are our strong beliefs."

Corbin believed, like his ancestors before him, that water and all life on Earth is a living entity, and we must reconnect with our Mother Earth by prayers, ceremony and talking to everything again.

All water comes from Mother Earth and that's her life-blood. Like humans, Mother Earth has a body and when it rains and water comes down from the mountains, it's like a human tear. Corbin prayed in the mornings for the sun, the air, the water, plants, the animals and the rocks. He reflected on the state of humanity. "We have to come back to the Native way of life. The Native way is to pray for everything. Our Mother Earth is very important. We can't just misuse her and think she's going to continue. We, the people, are going to have to put our thoughts together to save our planet here. We only have *One Water...One Air...One Mother Earth.*"

During Corbin's lifetime he witnessed trees dying, our rivers, lakes and oceans contaminated and our air toxic from pollution. He noted how humans were being affected by contaminates in our soil, water, milk and our food by the many types of cancers.

The indigenous Grandmothers tell the people to go to the oceans or rivers or the streams and call up the water spirits for healing and rebalancing. When you feel depressed, go to your Mother. Even water from your shower will help. We know from scientists that it is negative ions in the water that makes us feel better, and that's because we are Water Beings. We are related to all creatures, the whales, the dolphins, to all creation.

But now our oceans are dying and so are the sea creatures in it. Humans are overfishing the oceans and some scientists believe by the year 2050 our oceans will be devoid of fish. Coral reefs are dying worldwide from what is termed "bleaching." Coral reefs are needed to sustain the symbiotic relationship with unicellular protozoa that fish thrive on. Scientists believe "bleaching" is caused by acidification due to rises in carbon dioxide levels. Acidification also affects the corals' ability to create calcareous skeletons, essential to their survival.

There might be other factors causing coral decline in zooplankton levels as a result of overfishing, changes in water chemistry (acidification), increased sedimentation from silt runoff, herbicides, cyanide fishing, changes in salinity, elevated sea levels due to global warming, mineral dust from African dust storms caused by drought, and sunscreen from tourists swimming, snorkeling or diving in the ocean.

In the past few years the deaths of dolphins and millions of fish that have washed ashore on coastal beaches have baffled marine biologists. Whales, along with dolphins, are marine mammals of the Cetecea order. It is said they have great intellect and studies have confirmed they are telepathic. They seem to know something is happening to Mother Earth and they are responding.

On February 15, 2013, a "super mega-pod" of thousands of dolphins, more than 7 miles long and 5 miles wide, was spotted off the coastal waters of San Diego, California. That same day and time a superbolide meteor created by a near-Earth asteroid entered Earth's atmosphere over Russia at 09:20 a.m. Russian time with a speed of 42,900 mph. It quickly became brilliant as it flew over the southern Ural region of Russia. It was reported that the light from the meteor was brighter than the Sun, even at 100 km distance. The object exploded in an air burst over the Russian city of Chelyabinsk Oblast at 18.4 miles. The explosion was so great it produced a hot cloud of dust and gas and fragmentary meteorites as well as a huge shock wave that broke windows in the city of Chelyabinsk and injured many. It was estimated the shock wave was like 500 kilotons of TNT, 20-30 times more energy than the atomic bomb detonated over Hiroshima during World War II produced.

I don't think it's was a coincidence that the super mega-pod of dolphins were seen at exactly the time the Chelyabinsk meteor exploded over the Urals. They felt the shock wave go through the Earth and ocean and reacted to it. But how did they gather so quickly? They must have sensed the event long before it happened. Further evidence that our planet's creatures have a sixth sense and warn us before a catastrophic event if we understand the signs.

In 1993 and 1996 I visited Belize, in Central America, once home of the ancient Maya civilization. Belize is home to the rain forests, the Maya Mountains that tower over the country, white beaches, ancient Maya temples, blue ocean water and the home of blue holes, caverns of limestone created 65,000 years ago. Although I didn't have the opportunity to scuba dive in the great blue Hole off Belize's coast, I did swim in a smaller interior blue hole filled with spring water and tiny fish.

The Maya Mountains are the high, rugged core of Belize, composed of igneous, metamorphic, and sedimentary rocks that are from 125-320 million years old. The surrounding flat plains are underlain by Cretaceous and Tertiary rocks (1.6-65 million years old); largely lime stones that indicate that Belize was covered by a warm, shallow sea during this long period of time.

Scuba diving off Ambergris Caye in the coral reef was the most amazing experience for me. I swam beside huge grouper, barracuda, sting ray and a kaleidoscope of rainbow-colored tropical fish. Never have I felt such peace. The water spirits called out, guiding me through the water as I said a prayer of thanks while the tide tugged at me to go further out to sea. Instead of fighting the tide, and using up oxygen in my tank, I moved with it. The ocean had given me a life lesson—stop forcing things to happen in your life, be patience and all will come to you.

A few years later, I again discovered the power of prayer with the water spirits during a white river rafting trip on the white water of the Bruneau River located in southern Idaho. The Bruneau is considered one of the most beautiful desert river canyons with its towering cliffs that rival the Grand Canyon. The canyon has many species of birds including eagles and hawks, and other animals like rattle snakes, skunk, deer, badger, coyotes, bobcats and porcupine.

Normally the Bruneau is gentle, but an early snow melt in the high mountains had turned the river into raging Class IV rapids. News reports urged the inexperienced rafters to stay away, but my friends and I were determined to raft it anyway. I was confident about my seasoned river guide in our heavier Navy inflatable raft. Also joining us was well-known photographer Steve Snyder, from Ketchum, Idaho and another group of people that included Jack, his son Jeff and my longtime friend Lani. They had rented a light weight self-bailing raft. This was Lani's first rafting trip and she was extremely nervous about it.

On the first day our raft tipped over and we lost a few food supplies, but nothing major. On the third day as we approached Five-Mile rapids, one of the most treacherous rapids of the Bruneau, we put in to study the water conditions before attempting the ride it. Meanwhile, Jeff, his son and Lani were on the far side of the river when they caught an eddy and the boat overturned. All three of them were pulled into the churning water. Jeff and his son made it to the bank of the river, but my friend Lani disappeared, caught under the raft.

Suddenly she surfaced, gasping for air and fighting to get her head above water. We yelled for her to swim across the river so she wouldn't be pulled into the treacherous rapids. As I prayed to the water spirits and my spirit guides Lani suddenly found her strength and swam across the river to the bank where we pulled her to safely. This was an amazing and very humbling confirmation that water has consciousness—that our spirit guides/angels, and all of Mother Earth listens if we only take the time to pray and speak to them.

Healing Waters

As a child I've spent hours soaking in natural hot springs in Idaho, Utah and Nevada. The experience left my body and mind relaxed and stress free. Hot springs come from deep within Earth, deep within the planet for millions of years. Geothermal springs may hold healing properties due to the high mineral content (sometimes sulfur), magnetic properties and positive-charged ions. The benefits of "water healing," or hydrotherapy, have been recognized for thousands of years. In Europe, where hydrotherapy is especially popular, there are numerous health spas and health facilities for all types of "water cures." The heat from the hot springs can also improves circulation by causing blood vessels to dilate.

In the way the Qi, the life force gathers and pools at the surface of the human body at certain places along acupuncture meridians called "acupuncture points;" natural spring water also rises from Earth and pools at places known as hot springs and mineral baths.

My most memorable hot springs experience took place several miles from the town of Salmon, Idaho. In order to reach the hot springs visitors hiked three miles up a hill where the hot springs pours from the mountain and gathers into small pools on its way down from the top. The most extraordinary part of the hot springs were the hundreds of golden dragonflies flying around our faces and staring at us as if to say they were the guardians of the sacred water. We said a prayer to the water and dragonflies and continued to soak for two hours, laughing at the dragonfly's antics, watching the white billowy clouds float by and soaking up the healing waters. It was heavenly!

There are many stories of healing water and springs, but one of the most remarkable stories of healing water is found in Lourdes, France. The story of the healing water began on a cold, damp morning of February 11, 1858. Bernadette Soubirous, a young girl, and her younger sister Toinette and her cousin Jeanne Abadie went on an errand to gather firewood to warm the damp, cold room in which a meager meal would be prepared. When they reached an area called Massabielle, beyond the city limits, there was a large rock grotto formed by years of water erosion. It stood at the bottom of the mountain. Toniette and Jeanne had taken off their shoes and stockings to wade into a shallow portion of the canal to gather driftwood while Bernadette hesitated about crossing the icy water. She felt ill suddenly and called out to Jeanne to carry her across the water. The girls laughed at Bernadette's request as she removed her shoes and stockings.

At that moment Bernadette heard the sound of wind which startled her. She looked up, expecting to see the nearby poplar trees blowing, but instead they were motionless. She looked back at the grotto and noticed light as if the sun was reflecting off the water. But the day was cloudy and cold. As she stared, she noticed a woman standing in the midst of the glowing light. The Lady, wearing a blue sash around her dress, smiled at Bernadette.

Bernadette instantly reached for the Rosary beads in her pocket and tried to make the Sign of the Cross with them. That's when she discovered she couldn't move. It was like she was frozen in place. The smiling Lady instead made the Sign of the Cross with the Rosary she held in her hand. Only then was Bernadette able to do the same as The Lady motioned for her to come closer. Bernadette was too timid and remained in the same place. The lady had vanished and everything returned to normal.

Oddly, the two other girls had not seen anything except Bernadette praying.

Following The Lady's first apparition on Friday, February 11, 1858, Bernadette, felt herself pulled back to the grotto the next day after being reprimanded about her story. She eventually confided in a priest who was impressed with her strange account and asked if he could tell Abbe Peyramale, the pastor of Lourdes. Bernadette agreed.

Again Bernadette returned to the Grotto with the two girls and again the Lady waited with her peaceful smile. Bernadette kept sprinkling holy water they had brought with them as the Lady looked on with approval. The two girls could not see the Lady as Bernadette remained in a trance-like state. Realizing nothing would arouse her from her trance state, the girls ran for help. It took a man from the nearby mill to carry her back to the mill all the while she remained in the trance.

By February 18, two women asked Bernadette the Lady's name and what her intentions might be. They gave her a paper and pen and Bernadette extended them to her. Then she spoke to Bernadette. "It is not necessary." Then she asked if Bernadette would be gracious and visit her for fifteen days. She added, "I do not promise to make you happy in this world, but in the next."

Many began to notice the startling changes in Bernadette, but others began to question the validity of her story, including her father. On Monday, February 22, Bernadette disobeyed her parents and went to the grotto as she had promised the Lady. There was no vision that day.

On February 24, the Lady told her to pray to God for the conversion of sinners. The next day she was on her knees and moved to a certain spot in the grotto as if directed by an unseen hand and began digging with her hands. She racked the mud with her fingers and put her hands to her mouth to drink it. The gathered crowd was stunned, some believing she was crazy.

Only Bernadette heard the Lady say, "Go and drink at the fountain and wash yourself." After drinking the mud, Bernadette began to eat bits of a plant called *dorine* as directed by the Lady to forgiven the sinners of the world. Suddenly water began to bubble forth from the ground where Bernadette had dug only mud.

On Monday, March 1, hundreds of people had gathered at the grotto. Among them was Catherine Latapie, a mother of two small children. She was expecting her third arrival at any time. Nearly two years earlier she had fallen and broken her arm. The fall and broken arm left her with two fingers of her right hand paralyzed.

Catherine went to the spring while Bernadette went into a trance. There the woman plunged her right hand into the waters and at once warmth flowed through her entire arm, giving her a sense of well-being. When she withdrew her arm, her fingers, which had been doubled over, were completely straightened.

The excitement of the cure caused Catherine to go into labor.

Hours later, four miles from the grotto at the village of Loubajac, Catherine gave birth to a baby boy, who later became a priest. Catherine was the first of millions of people to be healed in the miraculous healing waters of Lourdes.

Another side note to the healing of Lourdes and other places visited by the Blessed Virgin Mary, people reported the strong scent of roses and witnessed rose petals falling from the sky. It is believed that Nostradamus, the sixteenth century prophet, astrologer and physician, used rose petals for curing the Black Death or bubonic plague the raged across Europe, spread by fleas and rodents. During the fourteenth century it is estimated that 75-200 million people died from the Black Death, a name given to the plague due to the way it caused gangrene in the extremities of the body.

Water Oracle

The Oracle of Delphi was an important shrine of Greece dating back to 1400 B.C. The Oracle was built around a sacred spring where it was considered to be the omphalos or center of the world.

People came from all over Greece and lands beyond to have their questions about the future answered by the Pythia, the priestess of Apollo. Her answer, although cryptic, could determine the course of everything from a farmer planting his seedlings to an empire declaring war. When someone was unhappy with the oracle's interpretation, the oracle was happy to provide another prophecy if more gold was paid.

The Oracle of Delphi was a showcase of art treasures. All Greek states would send rich gifts to keep the Oracle on their side. That all ended in the 4th century AD.

Magnetic Properties in Water

Water has magnetic properties. Dowsers have known this for centuries by using a divining rod or dowsing rod made of a forked branch from a tree or bush to locate ground water. Usually the best branch for dowsing is from the willow tree or peach tree. Often the branches are grasped palms down and the dowser walks slowly over the places he suspects the minerals or water and the rod

Earth Energy

begins to dip down, twitches or inclines as if pointing to the spot on the ground. This method is also known as "Willow Witching."

Paranormal energy and activity have been associated in buildings and land where water flows underground. Even Paranormal researchers have discovered high electromagnetic fields (EMF) in these paranormal active areas with their EMF detectors. According to Heather Woodward in her book, *Ghosts of Central Arizona,* originally EMF detectors were designed to locate manmade electromagnetic fields that are caused by electricity. Common sources for electromagnetic fields are computers, televisions, electrical outlets, kitchen appliances and also walkie-talkies and cell phones when in use. Although science can't prove that EMF detectors can pick up paranormal activity, the common theory suggests that a paranormal presence may disrupt an electromagnetic field by using it as an energy source to communicate.

I was a big fan of the paranormal SYFY television show *Ghost Mine,* where paranormal investigators Patrick Doyle and Kristen Luman joined nine miners in the remote woods of Sumpter, Oregon, once one of the richest gold mines in the United States. It was abandoned 80 years ago after a series of tragedies. The mine had a haunted reputation that Luman and Doyle wanted to investigate while miners worked it.

The episode that really fascinated me aired on September 11, 2013. Mikey, the son of one of the seasoned miners joined the crew. Mikey and another miner nicknamed Bucket worked to clear a debris barrier in an area known as the "Ballroom" deep within the mine. Something inexplicable happened to them one day. The men normally clocked out at a certain time in the evening but Mikey and Bucket were still missing by 6 o'clock that evening.

As the group went to find them Mikey and Bucket returned, confused and believing only an hour had passed when in fact they had been in the mine for seven hours. Stranger yet; they hadn't made much progress on clearing the debris barrier. Although electromagnetic energy is known to play tricks on the mind and cause disorientation, what caused the men to have amnesia? Where were they? Later the Ballroom was checked for oxygen levels and those readings proved to be normal but the EMF readings were high.

Could the mine be a stargate into another world like the infamous Bermuda Triangle where ships and planes simply vanished without a trace over the years? The miners claimed they didn't recall anything except working, but how could they have worked seven hours without accomplishing anything? Those hours vanished from their lives, leaving the miners bewildered and extremely frightened.

The Sumpter mine holds two elements strongly linked to paranormal activity—water and crystals.

Myths and Legends

There are legends of mighty civilizations that reached incredible advancement only to vanish beneath the sea. Even the Bible tells of a Noah building an ark to save as many species as possible before a flood of great magnitude covered the earth and destroyed the wicked.

Myths and legends arose of gods who ruled the seas. One such god of the sea was the Roman god Neptune. For the Greeks it was the god Poseidon who also ruled the water. He was one of the twelve Olympian deities of the pantheon in Greek mythology. His domain covered the oceans, and he is called the "god of the Sea." He was also referred to as "Earth-Shaker" due to his role in causing earthquakes.

The ocean and the vast seas have always held mysteries and danger for the seafarers who were courageous enough to challenge the water. They believed their gods would guide and protect them from sea serpents that lived in the oceans and waited to devour their ships.

Water Nymphs (Naiads)

Nymphs were female nature entities that were bound to a particular location or land. They were also known as Naiads and inhabited fountains, wells, springs, brooks, rivers, marshes, ponds and lagoons. The essence of a Naiad was bound to the water body she inhabited. If a spring dried, the Naiad within it died. Some stories depict Naiads as dangerous creatures, because they could take men underwater when fascinated by their beauty, and these men were never to be seen again. Naiads were known by their jealous nature. A naiad that was once cheated by her husband is said to have blinded him in revenge. In Greek mythology naiads were friendly creatures that helped sailors fight perilous storms. They also had the power of foresight, and were said to make prophecies.

Some other species of Naiad: Crinaeae lived in fountains, Limnades lived in lakes, Pagaeae lived in springs, Potameides lived in rivers, and Eleiomomae lived in marshes.

Mermaids

Mermaids were believed to be aquatic creatures with the upper body of a female human and the tail of a fish. Oddly, mermaids appeared in folklore of many cultures worldwide, including the Near East, Africa, Asia and Europe. The first stories go back to ancient Assyria where the goddess Atargatis transformed herself into a mermaid out of shame for killing her human lover. They were an omen associated with perilous events like floods, storms, shipwrecks and drowning. In some cultures the mermaid was benevolent, bestowing good luck and sometimes falling in love with humans.

Christopher Columbus reported seeing mermaids while exploring the Caribbean, and sightings have been reported in the 20th and 21st centuries in Canada, Israel and Zimbabwe.

Atlantis

The Green philosopher Plato first mentioned the fictional island of Atlantis in his works *Timaeus* and *Critias*. He said the land mass was once a vast naval power that had conquered parts of Western Europe and Africa. At the end of the story, Atlantis eventually fell out of favor with the gods and sank into the Atlantic Ocean. While some ancient writers viewed Atlantis as fictional, others believed it existed 9,000 years before Plato's time and might have come from Egyptian records. Atlantis supposedly existed in the middle of the Atlantic Ocean between Africa and America, and the people of Atlantis were highly advanced in war and navigating the ocean.

The psychic Edgar Cayce, (1877-1945), known as the sleeping prophet, provided 14,000 readings throughout his lifetime on healing, wars, visions of future, catastrophes, the life of Jesus, Atlantis, Lemuria, and the origins and development of the human race. Many of his predictions and curative remedies proved accurate while given in a hypnotic trance.

Some of the most puzzling of all Cayce's readings were the readings on Atlantis. Throughout his readings on Atlantis he stated it was the "first" civilization to be technologically superior to even our own technology, but misuse of technology caused its demise.

One interesting prediction Cayce made was about a new land appearing off the east coast of North America that was once Atlantis, which he called the "rising of Atlantis." It was during 1968 that the so-called "Bimini Road" was discovered in the Atlantic Ocean. The Bimini Wall or Road consists of flat-lying, tabular, and rectangular, sub-rectangular, polygonal and irregular block lying in shallow ocean water off the coast of Bimini in the Caribbean. The giant blocks are in 5.5 meters of water off the northwest coast of North Bimini island.

The Bimini Road, the largest of three linear features, is 0.8 km (0.50 mi) long, a northeast/southwest-trending feature with a pronounced hook at its southwest end. It consists of stone blocks measuring as much as 3–4 m (10–13 ft.) in horizontal dimensions, with the average size being 2–3 m (7–10 ft.). The larger blocks show complementary edges, which are lacking in the smaller blocks. Two narrower and shorter features, approximately 160 and 200 ft. long lie shoreward. The Bimini Road consists of smaller tabular stone blocks that are only 1–2 m (3–7 ft.) in maximum horizontal breadth. Having rounded corners, the blocks composing these pavements resemble giant loaves of bread made of limestone.

Archeologists and scientists continue to debate the significance of the stones and whether or not they were manmade or natural formations. So far the verdict is out.

Cayce said Atlantis disappeared somewhere in the Atlantic ocean some ten thousand years ago. The continent was the size of Europe, including Asia. Unlike Plato, Cayce said Atlantis was destroyed in three major periods with the first two geological events taking place around 15,600 B.C. when the mainland was divided into islands. Cayce named the three main islands of Atlantis—Poseida, Og and Aryan.

The Atlanteans had advanced so far in science they had harnessed the power of quantum worlds; this included the use of crystals and sound waves for healing, elevators, airships, and submarines. Atlanteans were adept at the use of the silicon chip at levels that surpass our modern twenty-first century technology. They had laser technology and memory chips. In their world they created monstrosities of half-man, half-animal through genetic engineering, used for slave labor. Cayce also stated the Atlantean scientists made extensive use of mental telepathy, psycho-kinesis and astral projection into fourth dimensional consciousness.

Cayce made an eerie comparison between our current world and that of Atlantis where the Children of the Law of One wanted to return to a more spiritual nature of life with the land, based on natural laws, while the other group, the Sons of Belial, wanted to exploit natural resources for material gain. Sound familiar?

Cayce stated in a trance-like state that many of the souls incarnating on Earth in the past one-hundred years lived on Atlantis and have returned to rectify the wrongs committed during that Atlantean lifetime, and those known as the Sons of Belial, have returned to commit their prior sins on the planet with total disregard for Earth.

Many of the dark-skinned Atlanteans managed to escape the deluge of their land, relocating to Egypt and South America where they brought records of their land and technology. Cayce revealed there are three locations where records of Atlantis will someday be discovered—but not until humans had reached a certain point in their spiritual evolution. Those three places exist in Egypt under the left paw of the Sphinx, in a submerged temple in the Caribbean, and in an ancient Yucatan temple.

Lemuria or Mu

Lemuria or Mu was a hypothetical lost continent that was located either in the Indian or Pacific Ocean. At present scientists have dismissed the existence of Lemuria as unlikely by researching plate tectonics, but Edgar Cayce and paranormal researchers believe it existed. Like Atlantis, the continent existed long before Atlantis, and sank beneath the ocean from geological changes.

Between 1923 and 1944 Edgar Cayce provided 700 readings on Atlantis and Mu, ancient America, and excursions into the Americas by those fleeing cataclysms in Atlantis. The readings also claimed that the mound builders of America resulted from multiple cultures which included groups from Atlantis, the

Yucatan, survivors from Mu, the Lost Tribes of Israel, the Norse, and native people of America.

Cayce's readings asserted that a portion of southwestern United States was occupied approximately 10 million years ago, a time when Earth's land mass was in great upheaval. But the beings of Mu were more of thought forms projected into primitive life than the present day human. Mu was west of the Americas. Its destruction occurred sometime around 50,000 B.C., an event Cayce described as the "first destruction" of Atlantis.

Interestingly enough, several underwater ruins of cities have been found off the coast of Japan and Okinawa, perhaps remnants of the ancient land of Mu.

The Bermuda Triangle

In an area in the Atlantic Ocean that covers a triangle-shaped area between Bermuda, Puerto Rico and Fort Lauderdale, Florida stories have been told for centuries of anomalies and unexplained disappearances of ships, boats, people, and planes. The area is nearly a million square miles wide, and extends from the Gulf of Mexico to the Caribbean Sea. Theories abound that the area violates the laws of physics and might be a stargate entrance for extraterrestrials.

However, skeptics contend the disappearances haven't been that many, and that most happened years earlier before radar and satellite could track lost ships or planes. They also claim the number of disappearances is relatively insignificant compared to the number of ships and planes that do pass through the area safely.

The ocean current within the Triangle is associated with violent weather, which would be a logical cause for any of the disappearances. Theories state the triangle has opposite magnetism, which interferes with GPS equipment and causes ships and planes to crash in reefs. Another explanation includes methane hydrate bubbles that could cause rapid sinking of ships in the Triangle by water density displacement. But that might not explain why airplanes have vanished over this area of the Atlantic Ocean and the reports of compass and magnet anomalies.

One of the most famous disappearances was Flight 19, a naval air force squadron. Flight 19 was a training flight with five TBM Avenger Bombers that was led by the commander Charles Taylor. There were 13 others in the flight (in different planes) but all were trainees. Taylor was the only experienced pilot.

On a clear December 5, 1945 day at 2:10 p.m., the five Avengers of Flight 19 took off one after the other from the Naval Air Station (NAS) of Fort Lauderdale at Florida for a routine training session. The weather over the route was reported as excellent, a typical sunny Florida day. At about 3:30 p.m., Taylor sent a message to the control tower that his compass was malfunctioning and he thought he was somewhere around the Florida Keys, which is a chain of islands in the south of Florida. So instead of heading towards East, he thought that they headed southwards due to compass problems.

At 3.45 p.m., Taylor's voice was heard again at the control towers. He sounded confused. "Cannot see land, we seem to be off course." At this stage there was another transmission that was picked up when one trainee student said to the other "If we would just fly west, we would get home."

The last transmission suggestions that the flight was not anywhere near the Bermuda Triangle. This might explain why the planes were never recovered. Although Taylor was an experienced pilot, he had a history of getting lost. During World War II he had to ditch his plane into the sea, and he was not familiar with the area around east and south of Florida.

So there's the possibility that Flight 19 became lost, ran out of fuel and had to ditch in the ocean where the crew would have died and their planes vanishing beneath the waves. All 14 airmen on flight were lost, as were all 13 crew members of a PBM Mariner flying boat assumed by professional investigators to have exploded in mid-air while searching for Flight 19.

For the disappearance of other flights, notably the Star Tiger, no explanation has been found and it still remains unclear why the wreckage of the planes was never recovered. It all began on January 30, 1948, the Star Tiger, a Tudor aircraft was on its way to Bermuda. The long 12 hours journey from Santa Maria in Azores was almost coming to an end. At 3:15 a.m., the radio operator of the aircraft received the radio position of the plane. It was all set to land at 5 a.m. in Bermuda. In just ninety minutes time the 25 passengers on board would see the marine lights of Bermuda, but that was the last the plane was ever heard of again.

Another mystifying case took place October 1972 on the Mary Celeste, a ship headed from New York to Genoa, Italy. The captain Benjamin Briggs, his wife and 2-year-old child and a crew of seven set sail carrying a cargo of 1,701 barrels of raw commercial alcohol valued at some $35,000 and had full insurance.

On December 4, 1872, a British Empire vessel named *Dei Gratia* found the Mary Celeste off the coast of Portugal. She apparently looked abandoned although still under sail. No one was on board, there was no sign of violence and none of the crew's personal belongings were taken, so piracy was ruled out. Also, ruled out—weather, an undersea earthquake, and rogue waves.

The Mary Celeste remains another Bermuda Triangle mystery.

Flight 441 became another Bermuda mystery. It was a huge carrier that belonged to the US Navy. The civilian or the commercial model of the aircraft is known as the Super Constellation. In military version, it was called R7V-1. The aircraft was one of the greatest successes of its time. It was hyped that it could cross the Atlantic in eight and half hours. On October 30, 1954, Flight 441 took off from the Patuxent River Naval Air Station bound for Lajes in Azores with 42 passengers, all naval officers and their families who were transported overseas.

Like other flight disappearances, at first there had been regular communication received from the aircraft, and then total silence. The last transmission was received around 11:30 p.m. which was a regular report informing its location. That time the aircraft was about 400 miles off the coast.

The disappearance of Flight 441 remains as one of the strangest mysteries of the Bermuda Triangle. There was never any clue on what happened to Naval flight—no wreckage. The incidence was thoroughly investigated by the board, which focused on the plane itself, the weather and the Pilot Leonard's capability. Here is what the board of investigation reported about the Pilot and the weather:

"...*Lt. Leonard has been flying the North Atlantic routes for the past two years and it is thought that he was very familiar with this kind of weather. His choice of 17,000 feet altitude for this flight was a good one. According to the weather cross section 19,000 feet would have been an even better altitude. At any rate he should have been on top, for the most part, except for occasional buildup. It must be pointed out that the R7V-1 was equipped with ASP-42 Airborne Radar and is always used when flying this sort of weather."*

Other areas that are known for disappearances and shipwrecks include Lake Ontario, the Formosa Triangle near Taiwan and an area known as the Japan Triangle. On March 8, 2014 Malaysia Airline Flight 370 and its crew and passengers of 239 vanished without a trace over the South China Seas. Speculation has ranged from hijacking, explosion of the ocean, aliens, stargates, and weather anomalies, but so far not one clue has surfaced.

I've included a few theories on the Bermuda Triangle and other triangle areas around the world:

Methane Gas trapped under the sea floor can erupt; as a result can lower the water density causing ships to sink. Even planes flying over it, can catch fire and get completely destroyed during such gas blowouts. The Bermuda Triangle area is known for undersea volcanoes and earthquake activity.

Sargasso Sea: Another strange area is the Sargasso Sea that has no shores and bound only by water currents on all sides. Many ships passing through it have been stranded and made motionless.

Electronic Fog: This is a strange thick cloud appears from nowhere and engulfs a ship or a plane. Suddenly instruments malfunction, and then the ship or the aircraft vanishes without a trace. It was in 1979, Canadian scientist John Hutchison had shown that if electromagnetic fields of different wave lengths interplay with each other, at some point there may be strange things happening like—water swirling in a cup, objects like wood or metal start rising from the floor and float around, or some objects can even shoot off at fantastic speed.

Stargates: Conspiracy theorists believe terrestrial stargates exist everywhere on the planet. Extraterrestrials can move in and out of our world through these stargates. Supernatural areas include the Bermuda Triangle, Mount Shasta in Northern California, the Dragon's Triangle, the Gulf of Aden, King Aramu

Muru's stargate near Peru's Lake Tiahuanaco, the Maya ruins in Mexico's Palenque, two in Egypt (Abu Ghurab and beneath the Giza Plateau), Uluru and Serpentine National Park in Australia, Mt. Kailash in Tibet, Machu Picchu in Peru, Sedona in Arizona, and Stonehenge in England.

Edgar Cayce stated in trance that the great Atlantean Crystal sank beneath the Atlantic Ocean during the time of upheaval. The crystal, a great power source for the Atlanteans, can activate at certain times of the year and under certain conditions. Cayce said the crystal was housed in a special oval-shaped building, with a dome that could be rolled back, exposing the Crystal to the light of the sun, moon and stars at the most favorable time. The interior of the building was lined with non-conducting metal or stone, similar to asbestos or bakelite, a thermosetting plastic.

The Crystal itself, the Tuaoi Stone, or Firestone, was huge in size, cylindrical in length, and prismatic in shape, cut with six sides. Atop the crystal was a moveable capstone, used to both concentrate incoming rays of energy, and to direct currents to various parts of the Atlantean countryside. The Crystal gathered solar, lunar, stellar, and atmospheric and Earth energies as well as unknown elemental forces and concentrated these at a specific point, located between the top of the Crystal and the bottom of the capstone.

The energy of the Crystal was used for various purposes, in different periods of Atlantean history. In the beginning, about 50,000 years ago, the Great Crystal was operated exclusively by the Initiates, or those spiritually advanced enough to handle such a tremendous source of power. Cayce in several of his readings stated that during this remote period in history, the Crystal was the development of a prehistoric wisdom which recognized that all energies in the universe are but aspects of One Energy, and one Mind.

As time progressed, however, and the Atlantean civilization matured further, the Crystal's energies were also utilized in rejuvenating the human body. The Atlanteans were able to live hundreds of years, yet always kept a youthful appearance. The Crystal became hot when in operation; it employed inductor methods; utilized a kind of wave energy other than electromagnetic; and it emitted an invisible beam of energy that could pass through water and solid matter.

Cayce spoke of *rays from the sun amplified by crystals* and *raising of the powers from the sun itself to a ray that makes for the disintegration of the atom. This in turn produced gases which "were used for what we call today the conveniences"—the motivative forces or radial activity, electrical combinations, the motivative forces of steam, gas and the like*. The Great Crystal could utilize *the concentration of energies that emanate from bodies that are on fire themselves, along with elements that are found and not found in the Earth's atmosphere*. Another Cayce reading stated, "The crystals made for the connections with the internal influences in the Earth."

American archaeologist and Research writer for Ancient American and Atlantis Rising magazines, William Michael Donato, believed that Cayce might have been describing a thermally excited gas laser with quartz housing. Quartz allows for the transmission not only of visible wavelengths but also ultraviolet and infrared radiations, unlike ordinary glass. It is both piezoelectric and pyro-electric.

From Cayce's readings, Donato concluded, *the force which came from the Tuaoi 'arose in the form of rays invisible to the eye,' suggesting ultraviolet or infrared as the operating range. An ultraviolet laser ionizes the air directly in front of the beam creating an electrically conducting pathway—literally sending electricity directly through the air without the use of wires, cables or other instruments. All that would be necessary to modify the beam for various uses and would be electro-optical like special mirrors and prisms.*

We can imagine smaller variants of the Tuaoi set in an airship, for example. The beam would transmit energy directly into these receptor crystals which would in turn re-amplify the power, possibly powering an electrical or thermal engine. We have done the same thing by shining laser light into another laser crystal.

According to Cayce, toward the end of the Atlantean existence they became enamored by their power to control and rule with the Crystal. The operation of the Crystal was taken over by those of less spiritual fortitude, and the energies of the Great Crystal were tuned to higher and more destructive frequencies. This in turn activated volcanoes and melting mountains, ultimately causing the submergence of Atlantis after several years. It may have also caused the Earth's axis to shift. In one specific reading, the psychic described how the Crystal energies were directed into the Earth, overloading the Earth energy grid system.

Does this sound like history repeating itself? If we believe Cayce and his story of the Great Crystal of Atlantis, and how a great number of Atlanteans have incarnated today, we can understand how our planet again is being destroyed by the same power-hungry people. Cayce predicted Earth would shift its axis again in the late twentieth century or early twenty-first century. Only time will tell is he was right.

John H. Sutton, a NASA researcher involved with applications of low energy plasmas, hypothesized that the Great Crystal described by Cayce was a "laser-infusion reactor/gravity wave generator." He suggested that when intense gravity waves were generated by the Crystal and beamed into the Earth, the planet's crystalline quartz—which occurs in granite rock averaging twenty-five percent throughout Earth's crust—absorbed the energy. The resulting meltdown of large masses of subterranean quartz would have been the triggering mechanism for causing major slippage along the Earth's fault-lines, destroying Atlantis and precipitating a global shift.

Interestingly enough, inventor, engineer, physicist and futurist, Nikola Tesla, (1856–1943), best known for his contributions to the design of the modern alternating current (AC) electricity supply system, was experimenting with certain frequencies and resonance. It is believe his experiment created an earthquake near his New York City laboratory. He also claimed his technology could split the Earth in half.

I've often wondered if Tesla recalled a prior Atlantean lifetime and utilized his advanced knowledge at the turn of the twentieth from that ancient time. There is an excellent book about the life of Nikola Tesla by Margaret Cheney, titled *Tesla: Man Out of Time,* about his futuristic (or perhaps ancient) genius.

Healing Water Exercise

Water contains negative-charged ions, especially free-flowing water like rivers and oceans. Visiting or living by water can be soothing and beneficial for the body, mind and soul.

If two or more conduct this exercise, the better. Find a stream, river, pond, lake, and ocean and place your hands above the water. If you can't get to a large body of water, a bowl of water in your home will suffice.

Speak to the water as if it is a conscious, sentient being (it is!) and tell the water your intentions to heal it of negative energy. Tell the water of your love and appreciation for its life-giving qualities. If you have crystals place them in the bowl of water or hold them above the water.

Stretch your consciousness to the twelfth chakra and take that light and focus it into the water. Singing, music and chanting can be incorporated which will generate a higher vibration in the area and in the water. Every person on this planet has the ability to reactivate the Living Library of Earth by mind, love, light and intentions for a higher good.

Visualize giant waves of light coming from the sun (light is knowledge) that flood the waters of Earth, purify the water spirit element and all of Earth. See the water and all fish and creatures that reside in water healed of toxins and becoming plentiful again. See the waters of the Earth clear and pure.

We are the dreamer beings who can manifest any thought or idea into reality.

Breathe in light and become the water. Feel its power. As you intend, pray and visualize a new world being born, feel your own body becoming lighter as you vibrate on a higher level, feel the joy and connectedness with your surroundings. Know that you are part of a grand purpose, and you are a powerful spiritual being that can dream a new world into being.

Prayer to Water by Western Shoshone Spiritual Leader Corbin Harney

Clean us, when we drink you.
Be good to us, so we'll have a healthier body.
Make sure you take are of what's out here, all the trees, all the living things that are on this Mother Earth, all the plant life, the birds, and so forth. Continue to flow clean, so that we have clean water to drink.

To the water that comes out of the ground, I am saying:

Be pure and clean, so that when we use you, you keep us healthy, and so you can continue to be clean for us and all the living things.

Make sure that when you come from within the Earth, make sure you're clean.

When we use you, when we drink you, make sure you give us strength and energy, and when we take a bath with you, I'm asking you, Water, to continue to give us a good feeling, with whatever we do with you, in whatever way we use you, so that all the living things, all the plant life, everything that uses you in any way, that everything can be clean.

Prayer to Rain by Corbin Harney

We have to get together like our forefathers did to bring moisture of some kind wherever the land is parched.

I ask for moisture to fall upon us so the grass will start to grow.

I pray for moisture for the things that survive on the grass, what we humans tromp down.

The food that all the creatures are supposed to eat, we tramp it down so it's flat on the ground.

So we know it's up to us; together we have to ask for the rain to come down, so the grass will continue to grow again.

> *Even some Indian people must be reminded of our four cardinal principles: respect for Wakan Tanka, respect for Mother Earth, respect for our fellow man and woman, and respect for individual freedom.* —Oglala Sioux Ceremonial Leader Ed McGaa "Eagle Man"

CHAPTER THREE
Earth Element

Gender - female, Color - green, Direction – North, and Season - Winter

Of all the four elements, Mother Earth has been worshipped as a living being, the provider to all life, down through the ages. Fifteenth-century alchemist Basilius Valentinus said, "The Earth is not a dead body, but is inhabited by a spirit that is its life and soul. All created things, minerals included, draw their strength from the Earth Spirit. This spirit is life, it is nourished by the stars, and it gives nourishment to all living things that it shelters in its womb."

Earth rules the north because it's always cold and dark there. The color for Earth is green, the color of plants and fields, and Earth's time of the year is winter, according to ancient wisdom.

In our modern world, humans have grown away from Mother Earth wisdom, entrenched in materialism and technology. In the nineteenth century, Smohalia, a Sioux Indian holy man, could see what was happening to humanity and expressed his sadness when he said: *You ask me to dig in the Earth? Am I to take a knife and plunge it into the breast of my mother? But then when I did she will not gather me again into her bosom...Then I can never enter her body and be born again. You ask me to cut the grass and the corn and sell them to get rich like the white men. But how dare I crop the hair of my mother?*

We have forgotten that we are made up of all of Mother Earth's elements, so we are her children, and she is our Mother. She is the dirt we walk on, the rocks that emerged from her womb, the mountains, canyons and valleys are her body and blood. Ancient and indigenous people have long known the healing effects of the planet, and have sought sacred places that hold energy.

The Australian Aborigines conceived rocks as the sources of the souls of newborn babies, and their ancestors "who passed that way in the dreamtime." Sometimes the only thing they say is, "You see that rock? It has power."

Ancient people have always known rocks and mountains possess great energy. Is it any surprise that megalithic structures were built worldwide by our ancient ancestors who incorporated the power of the stones? Stones were used as altars where worshippers communicated with the spirit of the stone by pouring oil or blood over it.

Blood signified a sharing of life while oil represented fertility and abundance of life. Sacred standing stones were not just a token that a place was frequented by a God, but a place where he consents to enter into stated relationship with humans. A pillar stone represented three cosmic regions—heaven, earth, and the underworld, and allowed mortals to access all three worlds.

Later in human history, groups of stone pillars were set up, including double pillars, as erected by the Phoenician culture. The pillars often served as a gateway to the world of the dead. In Megalithic times the pillar became the doorway to the temples and tombs, and also marked the solstices and equinoxes.

Stonehenge was the foremost Megalithic religious construction of rock. Although there is much debate over how Stonehenge's monolithic stones were cut and moved, the common theory is the solid bedrock was cut by water, frost and wind through the ages. All the Megalithic people had to do was shape them and move them to make their monuments.

Another famous sacred rock is found on the Temple Mount in Jerusalem, is the holiest site in Judaism, and a revered site to Christians. According to the Bible (Genesis 22:1-14), God told Abraham to bring his son, Isaac, to the land of Moriah meaning "Chosen by Yah") and offer him as a sacrifice on the mountain. As Abraham was about the complete the killing of his beloved son, God stopped him and provided a ram as a substitute sacrifice.

Through the ages humans have claimed they can get in touch with some physical energy from the rocks. There is evidence that the energy comes from ley lines throughout the world. In China they are labelled "Green Dragon" (yang) and "White Tiger" (yin by the feng-shui).

Francis Hitching, a member of the Royal Institute of Archaeology, spent considerable time investigating megalithic stone monuments in the United Kingdom. He believed that the power of stones has "something to do with electromagnetism...it may have something to do with the unique qualities of quartz, which seems to be constituent of every active stone. The molecular structure of quartz is spiral. It is also piezo-electric: that is, it expands slightly if given a slight charge of electricity. If placed under pressure—as it would be if charged while inside another stone—alternate edges of its prism give off positive and negative voltages on what can reach a dramatic scale: a force of 1,000 pounds applied on each face of a half-inch crystal of quartz crates 25,000 volts."

As a child I learned that striking two quartz crystals together produces an electrical charge inside the quartz—piezoelectricity. (Please don't try this without using protective eyewear as crystals can splinter).

Scientists have long speculated that shamans may feel the power of a place" because of a number of factors relating to changes in the Earth's local magnetic field causing changes in electrostatic field strength and with negative ion concentrations.

There are stories of experienced rock climbers feeling strange and unexplainable effects from rocks. Dolores LaChapelle related this story from her *Earth Wisdom* book, "Once, in Canada, trying a rarely climbed route, I had been leading up a fairly difficult pitch when I came to a level spot with a very easy chimney going on up. But I could not bring myself to step up onto the first foothold (which was as easy as taking a step up a stairway). I tried a couple of times, but simply could not do it. Thinking I must be tired, I told the second rope to take over the lead. No sooner had the first man moved into the chimney when the whole thing avalanched out. He was not seriously hurt but was shaken. I had no way of explaining what I felt, but now, years later, I think it may possibly have had something to do with the pressure generated inside the rocks pushing against one another."

Rocks are part of ancient rituals still performed today. In Tibet, a traveler crossing the high mountain passes must leave a rock on the cairn at the top. Rocks are focal points for meditation in Zen gardens. Lakota Holy Man John Fire Lame Deer (1903-1976) said, *"Inyan*—the rocks are holy. Every man needs a stone to help him. Also you are always picking up odd-shaped stones, pebbles and fossils, saying that you do this because it pleases you, but I know better. Deep inside you there must be an awareness of the rock power, of the spirits in them, otherwise you would not pick them up and fondle them as you do."

My teacher Oglala Sioux Ceremonial Leader Ed McGaa "Eagle Man" says Oglala people believe in the omnipotence of *Wakan Tanka* and wear or carry a small, spherical stone carefully rolled up in a wad of sage and deposited neatly in a miniature buckskin pouch no more than an inch in diameter.

According to author William K. Powers sacred stones play an important part of Oglala ritual and belief. The early chroniclers of the Sioux religion made numerous references to the importance of sacred stones in a variety of rituals that predate Yuwipi, or the spirit-calling ceremony.

Ancient temples and pyramids worldwide are testament of man's fascination with giant stones. But why was ancient man so fascinated with stones and giant structures that reached toward the heavens like mountains? Perhaps it's because concentrated energy exists in the apex of a mountain or any structure that goes to a point. There's a greater concentration of negative-charged ions, and it is believe that because there is less oxygen on mountain tops it can cause hallucinations and visions.

The Teotihaucán, Aztec and Toltec people tell of a flying,

feathered serpent, Quetzalcoatl, who could travel between Earth and the sky, bringing great knowledge to the people of Earth. Ancient myths suggest the ancient city of Teotihuacán, established in 100 B.C. and located in the Valley of Mexico 30 miles northeast of modern-day Mexico City, were constructed with the help of star beings from the Pleiades constellation, who gave them their DNA to advance human evolution.

It is said that Teotihuacan's city layout strangely resembles a computer circuit board with two large processor chips—the Sun Pyramid and the Moon Pyramid. Another strange discovery is the large quantities of Mica found in every building, yet the mineral is found 3,000 miles away in Brazil. The truly fascinating part about the Mica is that the mineral is stable when exposed to electricity, light, moisture and extreme temperatures. It has superior electrical properties as an insulator and as a dielectric, and can support an electrostatic field while dissipating minimal energy in the form of heat. It is also thermally stable to 500° C.

Archaeologists were baffled by the discovery of hundreds of once-metallic spheres buried deep beneath an ancient pyramid in Mexico City. Along the "Avenue of the Gods, the pyramids align in perfect distance in relationship to the orbits of our planets in our solar system and the large Pyramid of the Sun is positioned at the center of the other stone structures like our sun is at the center of our solar system and the planets revolve around it.

Teotihuacan means "City of the Gods." So we know that these ancient people had incredible knowledge in mathematics, geology, astronomy and engineering, but where did all this technological knowledge come from—from Star beings?

During a recent return visit to Mesa Verde National Park in Southwestern Colorado I was overpowered by a sense of déjà vu, as if I had lived there before in a previous lifetime. At the Cliff Palace at Mesa Verde National Park as I stood next to a deep kiva and felt the powerful energy I almost fell into the deep well. Luckily, my husband was next to me and caught me in time.

The Anasazi or Puebloans built kivas, a room used for religious rituals, ceremonies and gatherings associated with the Kachina belief system. The kivas at Mesa Verde are subterranean round rooms; however there are some kivas above ground. My sense was the kiva represented the womb of Mother Earth, and those inside were symbolically returning to the center. Native people knew that everything was round—the moon, the sun, the sky, the seasons and the stars, and even in the animal kingdom they witnessed birds build round nests. Life was a circle.

Cliff Palace at Mesa Verde National Park, Colorado

Sacred Circles

The Native American Medicine Wheel or Sacred Hoop was used for various spiritual and ritual ceremonies, especially for healing illnesses. It was believed that illness spring forth from spiritual imbalance. Most medicine wheels have a basic pattern with a center stone having spokes that radiate out from the center consisting of the four cardinal directions, as well as Father Sky, Mother Earth, and Spirit Tree, and four sacred colors of blue (north), yellow (east), black (west), white (south), and the center represent self and balance.

The four cardinal directions and four sacred colors represent the following properties:

Blue (north) is winter, going within self. Element: wind and breath.

Yellow (east) is spring and re-awakening time, growth. Element: Fire.

Black (west) is death and autumn, end of life's cycle. Element: Earth.

White (south) is peace and summer, a time of abundance. Element: Water.

Center is self. The beginning of all life. The symbolism can vary from tribe to tribe.

Oglala Sioux holy man Black Elk (1863-1950) said this about the circle:

"You have noticed that everything an Indian does in a circle, and that is because the Power of the World always works in circles, and everything and everything tries to be round.

"In the old days all our power came to us from the sacred hoop of the nation and so long as the hoop was unbroken the people flourished. The flowering tree was the living center of the hoop, and the circle of the four quarters nourished it. The east gave peace and light, the south gave warmth, the west gave rain and the north with its cold and mighty wind gave strength and endurance. This knowledge came to use from the outer world with our religion.

Everything the power of the world does is done in a circle. The sky is round and I have heard that the Earth is round like a ball and so are all the stars. The wind, in its greatest power, whirls. Birds make their nests in circles, for theirs is the same religion as ours. The sun comes forth and goes down again in a circle. The moon does the same and both are round. Even the seasons form a great circle in their changing and always come back again to where they were.

"The life of a man is a circle from childhood to childhood, and so it is in everything where power moves. Our teepees were round like the nests of birds, and these were always set in a circle, the nation's hoop, a nest of many nests, where the Great Spirit meant for us to hatch our children."

Holy Man Black Elk

It's interesting to note that domed structures have been found to be resistant to powerful winds compared to a typical square ranch or two-story home, plus they are more energy efficient. Native Americans and ancient people worldwide understood this concept of round thousands of years ago by observing their world and building round structures: igloos, teepees, kivas, Celtic round houses, mound builders, Stonehenge, and yurts.

Obviously, modern humans continue to ignore what works in best in nature when it comes to our homes and buildings.

Mountain Energy

Most people assume singer/songwriter John Denver wrote the song *Rocky Mountain High* about getting high on marijuana, but they'd be completely wrong. His song was about the mountains, Mother Nature and his experience one night. Denver started writing this song during the Perseid Meteor Shower which happens every August. He was camping with friends at the tree line at Williams Lake near Windstar (his foundation in Colorado) and all of a sudden there were many shooting stars and he noticed "The shadow from the starlight"... thus the line from the song. He says that while the inspiration struck quickly, it took him about nine months to complete the song. In Denver's autobiography, he wrote: "I remember, almost to the moment, when that song started to take shape in my head. We were working on the next album and it was to be called, *Mother Nature's Son,* after the Beatles song, which I'd included. It was set for release in September.

"In mid-August, Annie and I and some friends went up to Williams Lake to watch the first Perseid meteor showers. Imagine a moonless night in the Rockies in the dead of summer and you have it. I had insisted to everybody that it was going to be a glorious display. Spectacular, in fact.

"The air was kind of hazy when we started out, but by ten p.m. it had grown clear. I had my guitar with me and a fishing rod. At some point, I went off in a raft to the middle of the lake, singing my heart out. It wasn't so much that I was singing to entertain anyone back on shore, but rather I was singing for the mountains and for the sky. Either my voice gave out or I got cold, but at any rate, I came in and found that everybody had kind of drifted off to their individual campsites to catnap.

"We were right below the tree line, just about ten thousand feet, and we hadn't seen too much activity in the sky yet. There was a stand of trees over by the lake, and about a dozen aspens scattered around. Around midnight, I had to get up to pee and stepped out into this open spot. It was dark over by those trees, darker than in the clearing. I looked over there and could see the shadow from the starlight. There was so much light from the stars in the sky that there was a noticeable difference between the clearing and everywhere else. The shadow of the starlight blew me away. Maybe it was the state I was in. I went back and lay down next to Annie in front of our tent, thinking everybody had gone to sleep, and thinking about how in nature all things, large and small, were interwoven, when swoosh, a meteor went smoking by. And from all over the campground came the awed responses "Do you see that?" It got bigger and bigger until the tail stretched out all the way across the sky and burned itself out. Everybody was awake, and it was raining fire in the sky."

All my life I have experienced that same euphoria in the mountains that John Denver felt. I was blessed to have parents that loved the wilderness areas of the Northwest. My father loved to fish and hunt, so we camped beside Red Fish Lake in the Sawtooth Mountains or took trips to Idaho's South Hills, a few miles from Twin Falls. Mountains, for me, have a certain mystical quality and energy and that's why indigenous people sought them out. As a small child I remember telling my mother that when I grew older

I'd climb every mountain and find out what was on the other side. Needless to say, I never did climb every mountain but I have climbed quite a few of them in Idaho.

Besides natural mountains holding enormous amount of energy, it appears that ancient people discovered that artificial structures held great energy like the Maya temples found in Mesoamerica, the temple-mountain of Borobudur, the Mesopotamia ziggurats, and the Egyptian pyramids of Giza.

It is theorized that mountains and human-made mountains collect more solar energy and more cosmic ray energy from space than the surrounding land. Around mountain tops, positive ions, those which have lost an electron, are pulled towards the mountain by means of the Earth's force field and then move on down the mountain leaving the negative ions behind as they tend to move upward into the atmosphere. Most often, mountain tops have a larger concentration of negative ions—the calming and healing ones for humans.

Hippocrates noticed some 2,300 years ago that his patients benefited from certain kinds of air. He ordered them to take long walks by the sea or in the mountains. Shaman and holy people have always sought tall mountains to pray, beseech the elements and ancestors and seek powerful visions.

Jack Wetherford wrote in his book, *Genghis Khan and the Making of the Modern World*, a description of Mongol's Emperor Genghis Khan (1162-1227), and his spiritual powers. "Unlike the other steppe tribes that have embraced the scriptural and priestly traditions of Buddhism, Islam, or Christianity, the Mongols remained animists, praying to the spirits around them. They worshipped The Eternal Blue Sky, and then the Golden Light of the sun and the myriad of spiritual forces of nature.

"The Mongols divided the natural world into two parts, the Earth and the sky. Just as the human soul was contained not in the stationary parts of the body but in the moving essences of blood, breath, and aroma, so, too, the soul of the Earth was contained in its moving water. The rivers flowed through the Earth like the blood through the body and three of those rivers began here on this mountain. As the tallest mountain Burkhan Khaldun, it literally means, "God Mountain," was the khan of the area and it was the earthly place closest to the Eternal Blue Sky; and as the source of three rivers, Burham Khaldun was also the sacred heart of the Mongol world.

"For the Steppe tribes, political, worldly power was inseparable from supernatural power since both sprang from the same source, the Eternal Blue Sky. In order to find success and to triumph over others, one must first be granted supernatural power from the spiritual world. For his Spirit Banner to lead to victory and power, it had to first be infused with supernatural power. Temujin's three days of prayer while hiding on Burkhan Khaldun, marked the beginning of a long and intimate spiritual relationship he'd maintain with this mountain and the special protection he believed it provided. This mountain would be the source of his strength."

Oglala Sioux ceremonial leader Ed McGaa shared his spiritual experiences in his books, *Native Wisdom, Mother Earth Spirituality,* and *Rainbow Tribe.*

"One time, I, Eagle Man, had a medicine person put me up on the hill. Another time, I had two very powerful medicine people as my mentors. They simply said, 'Go up on this place, and vision quest.' They never accompanied me, nor did they have a sweat lodge waiting for me. They just took me up on the hill and placed me. They told me to do it and I just did it.

"I went to the mountain, and I parked my car down below. I took my peace pipe, and I simply walked up to the top of the mountain. In those days, believe it or not, when you went to Bear View Mountain, there was nobody there. Now it's quite crowded because Native spirituality has become so popular. But when I used to go there, I would be the only one on the whole mountain. So, I'd walk way up there and I'd fast. I'd drink no water. I'd simply take four little flags—red, white, black, and yellow--and place them around me, in a square. I'd stay in the square. If I had to go to the bathroom, I'd go away, of course, and then come back. But that's it. I'd sit in my square, and watch the sun come up in the morning, and set at night. I'd see the moon come up, and I'd see all the phases of the Earth. When you're fasting, your mind becomes more alert. You simply contemplate your life. And when you fall asleep, your dreams become more vivid.

"As each day goes by, the phases of life go through their cycles. At night, the stars come out. Pleiades [constellation] will actually dance for you if you're a vision quester. They light up, almost like a neon sign. I know people find that hard to believe, but that's just the mystery of the ceremony. An eagle will hover right over you knowing that you're in ceremony. Thunder and lightning come by, and you just endure it. It's no problem. Lightning can be flashing all around you, and you'll laugh. The Great Spirit is not going to take your life up there while you are vision questing. And if it does, who cares? You're in a good state. But you don't fear nature or God. The Great Spirit made you. Why should you fear it? You become more confident once you follow this natural road.

"So, this is an Eagle Man vision quest. It's performed by you and it's for yourself. You don't have to go through anybody. You can communicate to the Great Spirit through observation. Of course, it's nice to have a medicine person there to help you interpret the experience. When I came down from the mountain, the medicine man asked me, 'What did you see?' I said that I didn't see too much. 'This eagle just came and hovered over me, and lightning cracked close to me.' 'Were you afraid?' he asked? 'No, I wasn't afraid. In fact, I laughed. And I saw four horses before I went up the mountain. But they were real, live horses.' 'What color were they?' he wanted to know. He was even interested in these pre-vision quest scenes, as well as my dreams."

Ed McGaa has conducted a large number of sacred sweat lodges around the world and always conducts ceremony with thirty or less people in attendance, unlike the large sweat lodge held in Sedona, Arizona in 2009 that resulted in the death of three participants. People paid $10,000 to participate in James Ray's retreat. Ed has never charged for ceremony and never will. He also ensures that each participant is feeling well enough to endure the heat, and opens the flap from time to time to cool the air.

In Eastern philosophy, mountains are considered sacred and divine with supernatural powers. It is believed Gods and deities reside in them. Holy men and yogis have sought mountains for centuries to attain what is known as Nirvana, or enlightenment.

In the award-winning documentary, *Talking story: One Woman's Quest to Preserve Ancient Spiritual and Healing Traditions,* by filmmaker Marie-Rose Phan-Le, she tells of her journeys to Peru, Hawaii, Vietnam, Nepal, India and China to document local healing practices, in hopes of preserving some of the ancient wisdom of shaman and medicine people. While in the Himalayan Mountains near northwestern Nepal with photographer Thomas L. Kelly, her film crew and spiritual dhamis, Marie-Rose had a frightening out-of-body experience, a natural phenomenon for the local dhamis who allow a deity to take over their body to facilitate a healing.

In her book by the same name, *Talking Story*, Marie Rose described what happened next in the high altitude mountain village of Bargaun.

"I had been feeling unwell all day with nausea and a persistent headache, so as Cora and I reflected on how fulfilling the trip had been despite its many challenges, we both agreed we were ready to move on from Humla. After we finished packing our things, we were leisurely strolling to gather the men, when all of a sudden I fell to the ground. I hadn't tripped or stumbled, but rather it was as if someone had knocked my legs out from under me. I was light-headed, confused, and had difficult speaking clearly. I didn't know what was happening, but I knew I was in trouble and needed help. In halting speech, I pleaded with Cora to call for the dhamis."

Once her team and the dhamis showed up, she remembered being collapsed on the ground on the upper level of Tsering's home and sobbing uncontrollably. Thomas Kelly and Cora, an assistant, held onto her back and shoulders to steady her. The next few moments were hazy, but the film crew captured the entire episode.

It is normal for mountain climbers to experience nausea, headaches, and light-headedness going from a low altitude to an altitude of 10,000 feet or more. It's called, "Acute Mountain Sickness," and certainly Marie-Rose had all the symptoms. She didn't have time to acclimate to the extreme altitude. Thomas believed she was having an epileptic fit due to her shaking, her bulging eyes and her veins popping out. The dharmis were also deeply concerned about her condition, but quickly it became clear to them this wasn't altitude sickness.

Dhami Mangale called for holy water from Lake Manasrovar. Tsering poured some of the water into Marie-Rose's mouth and into her cupped hands. She was lucid enough to understand their instructions to hold her hands out for the water and then she took big gulps, splashing the rest over her face and neck. Suddenly she began speaking in an unknown language. She was then hoisted on the back of Rinochinpo, the smallest guide, and carried down a wooden ladder to the ceremonial area. Everyone then scrambled to prepare her for an exorcism to rid her of whatever they believed has possessed her. Dhami Mangale rang his bell and started to chant to invoke the helpful deities. Whipcords lashed at her and barley grains were thrown at her.

When they assessed the exorcism had failed, Tsering and the dhamis concluded it was not an evil spirit that had invaded her body.

As Tsering beseeched the deity to leave her body, a voice with strength and power came through Marie-Rose and said, "He doesn't tell me when I've had enough. I'll leave soon. She's fine. We appreciate his concern for this one. We are not angry." She then took Tsering's and Dhami Mangale's hands and said she was giving them some of her power, so that they may be strengthened in their commitment to lead others with the purity of their hearts. After Tsering promised that the dhamis would pass on her message of spreading positivity and vanquishing jealous, dishonesty, and darkness, Marie-Rose was jolted back into her body.

It could be said the Marie-Rose inherited the ability to channel from a line of healers in her family, but she prefers not to deal with channeling at this time because it requires much time and learning and she also feels she'd rather devote her healing ability to this side of reality. Today, Marie-Rose continues her family heritage as a healer in Hawaii.

Marie Rose experienced what shamans have long known—mountains are sacred and gateways to other worlds. Do deities and spirits inhabit the mountains of the world or is there a more scientific explanation? I'd prefer to believe that our ancestors were right—that deities and increased geomagnetic energy reside on Mother Earth's majestic mountains.

Mount Everest in the Himalayas is Earth's highest mountain with an altitude of 29,029 feet above sea level. Hundreds of climbers have lost their lives on Mount Everest climbing to the top from frigid temperatures, low oxygen, slipping and fallings. There are also a large number of people who have simply vanished off the mountain and never found again. Those who die on the mountain are typically left there. So far 150 bodies have never been recovered. The Sherpa guides hired to lead climbers up Mount Everest believe that the mountain is blessed with a deities or spiritual energy. They warn all who climb Everest to show reverence when passing through this sacred landscape. Here, the karmic effects of one's actions are magnified, and impure thoughts must be avoided.

Dr. Mikao Usui (1865-1926), originator of Reiki energy, was reported to have meditated at the top of a mountain outside of Kyoto, Japan for 21 days. On the last day of the meditation Dr. Usui had a spectacular epiphany experience during which he was shown how to activate the energy and give the gift of Reiki, healing by laying on of hands. Usui then came down the mountain performing miraculous healings. After consulting with his mentor, he later set off into the world doing good works, teaching Reiki, and healing the infirm with his newly-given gift, all the while learning many important lessons about human nature.

Although Dr. Usui's spiritual enlightenment at the top of a mountain was never verified, his story is a reminder of Jesus climbing a mountain with his disciples to single out twelve choices and the story of Moses who climbed Mount Sinai and received the Ten Commandments by God.

Cave Energy

Ancient man sought caves for spiritual enlightenment and for protection. Many churches in Europe were built over caves, and catacombs and caverns lie beneath the Egyptian pyramids of Giza. In December 2009, after denying that they existed, Egypt's leading Egyptologist, Dr Zahi Hawass, admitted that an excavation team under his charge investigated an ancient tomb at the center of claims regarding the *alleged* discovery of a cave underworld beneath the Pyramids of Giza.

This is a surprising announcement for several reasons, not the least being that the "alleged" cave system has already been explored and photographed by British writer and explorer Andrew Collins. In August 2008, Collins announced that he had rediscovered the entrance to a previously unexplored cave system, entered via a mysterious tomb several hundred meters west of the

Great Pyramid. Perhaps it was how Collins discovered the cave entrance that has caused the controversy.

This discovery gives rise to Edgar Cayce's deep trance information that the Atlantean Hall of Records were buried under the Sphinx and housed incredible records about the lost continent of Atlantis and its demise over 10,000 years ago. Cayce said the temple records in Egypt could be entered by a hall or passageway that begins at or near the Sphinx's paw.

Could the darkest recesses of our planet contain important information left by our ancient ancestors left inside cave or caverns? Is there evidence of otherworldly contact with Earth's mysterious caves? Throughout human history, some caves have been considered sacred places for spiritual enlightenment, while others have been feared as portals or gateways to dark worlds where strange beings exist and kidnap humans. One can only imagine how these subterranean places influenced religions around the globe. Could some of Earth's deepest caverns be secret conduits to supernatural realms or gateways to other dimensions? In Charama, India, archaeologists recently discovered 10,000 year-old prehistoric artwork of what appeared to be extraterrestrial astronauts. Some ancient astronaut theorists speculate the ancient paintings to be visual records of alien encounters in the distant past. Is it possible that sacred wisdom is stored in crystals and minerals that cover the walls of caves? Quartz crystal can store information and has memory.

Quartz is the most common mineral on Earth and also the most varied. If the Australian Aboriginal elder Alinta was right, the minerals and quartz within our planet hold the energy grid together and keep it balanced. Quartz and other minerals have been used in many cultures as tools for divination of higher knowledge and sacred ceremony. Druid priests, Tibetan monks and Native Americans held crystals as sacred power objects.

In 2000 a mining operations exposed an extraordinary find when they were pumping water of a 30-by-90 foot cave near the town of Delicias in Northern Mexico. They uncovered giant crystals, known today as Mexico's Cueva de los Cristales (Cave of Crystals) that contains some of the world's largest known natural crystals—translucent beams of gypsum as long as 36 feet.

Giant Crystals of Delicias, Mexico

It is believed the Shroud of Turin, a linen cloth bearing the image of Jesus with wounds from the crucifixion happened inside the cave where he was entombed after death. Theorists believe a burst of energy took place in the cave and transferred his image onto the cloth when he ascended to heaven. There is great debate whether or not the Shroud is a medieval forgery or the cloth that covered Jesus. What is so interesting about the cloth is it appears to be a black-and-white negative, as if some great energy was imprinted on the cloth.

In 1978 a detailed examination carried out by a team of American scientists called the Shroud of Turin Research Project (STURP) found no reliable evidence of how the image was produced. In 1988 a radiocarbon dating test was performed on small samples of the shroud. The laboratories at the University of Oxford, the University of Arizona, and the Swiss Federal Institute of Technology concurred that the samples they tested dated from the Middle Ages, between 1260 and 1390. The validity and the interpretation of the 1988 tests are still contested by some statisticians, chemists and historians. According to Professor Christopher Ramsey of the Oxford Radiocarbon Accelerator Unit in 2011, "There are various hypotheses as to why the dates might not be correct, but none of them stack up." The shroud is kept in the royal chapel of the Cathedral of Saint John the Baptist in Turin, northern Italy.

In the Baian-Kra-Ula mountains in China in 1938, a scientific expedition led by Dr. Chi Pu Twi made an astonishing discovery that stunned the world. In caves perched high atop the mountain they found the occupants of an ancient culture. Buried in the dust of the cave floor lay 715 stone-like discs that was similar to that of a phonograph record, but ancient—10,000 to 12,000 years old. The spiral grooves that encompassed the disc proved to be more important than first believed; the groove itself was actually composed of tiny hieroglyphics that tell the incredible story of spaceships from other space, from some far off distant world, that crash landed in the mountains.

Theorists like Erich von Däniken and Peter Kolosimo believed the discs were actual records of an abortive space mission by alien astronauts 12,000 years ago. Further exploration of the interlinked caves lead by Professor Chi Pu Twi discovered several ancient and nearly arranged burial sites. Within the mound lay the skeletal remains of what was thought to be very strange race of human-like beings. They were approximately 4 feet tall and unnaturally frail and thin with large over-developed skulls. However, the professor was quick to point out that no one has ever heard of any known species of gorilla burying their dead.

Carved throughout the cavern on walls and ceilings were pictograms of the heavens: the sun, moon, stars and Earth. Each pictogram was connected by a series of dots that formed what looked like a map of the outer galaxy. But the height of the discovery were the disc, half-buried in the dirt floor of the cave.

The discs became known as the Dropa stones. It took 20 years before experts were able to decipher the 'speaking grooves.' In 1962, Dr. Tsum Um Nui broke the code, but the meaning of the discs were kept for only a few. The Peekjing Academy of Pre-History forbade him to publish his findings, but somehow Dr. Tsum Um Nui did publish his findings and entitled it, "The Grooved Script Concerning Spaceships which as Recorded on the Discs, landed on Earth 12,000 Years Ago."

"Were the Dropa really visitors from some distant planet, or is the story merely a creation myth imagined by a primitive culture? If the latter is true, it adds another "myth" to the large number of stories that ancient cultures had descendants from the heavens. And if the former is true, the Dropa stones could represent the first recorded visit of an alien civilization to our planet.

In New England there are secret sites that consist of stone chambers and monuments of various styles and sizes. Some historians say they are only 'root cellars' that were built by colonists, but others maintain the idea that these lithic sites were constructed by much earlier visitors. The fact that many of them seem to be aligned with astronomical should give one pause. Archaeo-astronomer Byron Dix determined that New England is chock-full of underground chambers. According to Mr. Dix there are 105 astronomically aligned chambers in Massachusetts, 51 in New Hampshire, 41 in Vermont, 62 in Connecticut, 12 in Rhode Island, and 4 in Maine. The Early Sites Research Society which has been studying the chambers for over three decades, claims to have documented over 400 chambers in New England. Mystery Hill, and Gungywamp are the only sites that are commercially available to the public, while the rest remain hidden on private land or from public knowledge.

These stone chambers come in many style but it's the beehive-shaped chambers that are the center of the debate. Some believe these structures resemble those built in Ireland by a certain order of Irish Monks. That is why they are called Monk Caves. Some of them are simple single chambers built into hill sides or as a dirt covered mound. Others have multiple chambers with entrance tunnels as long as sixty feet or more. Over time many of them have become over grown with trees and shrubs.

California is known for its caverns, and some of them are quite extensive. American explorer, Captain Ives William Walker, claimed he made a startling discovery in 1850. He supposedly discovered a city about a mile long with the lines of the streets and the positions of the buildings still visible, situated in Death Valley on the Nevada-California borders. At the center was a huge rock, between 20 to 30 feet high, with the remains of an enormous structure atop it. The southern side of the rock and the building were melted and vitrified as if a terrible explosion had taken place there. Walker assumed a volcano had created the strange glass but none existed in the vicinity. Tectonic heat could not have caused the liquefaction of the rock surface.

Later an associate of Captain Walker followed up his initial reports and said, "The whole region between the rivers Gila and San Juan is covered with remains. The ruins of cities are to be found there which must be most extensive, and they are burnt out and vitrified in part, full of fused stones and craters caused by fires which were hot enough to liquefy rock and metal. There are paving stones and houses torn with monstrous cracks [as though they had] been attached by a giant's fire-plough."

The Piute Indians have a legend of an ancient city that existed beneath Death Valley inhabited by a race of people they named, Hav-musuvs. In 1948, Native American Oga-Make related his account of a tribal secret held by the Paiute Indians who inhabited the Great Basin and the Mojave deserts of Utah, Nevada and California in a magazine which carried numerous articles on the mysterious "signs" and "fires" in the skies from the flying ships. He also related the legend of a people who lived thousands of years before the white man set foot in North America.

Oga-Make said the ships were being seen in the sky again, and he wondered if he should keep his knowledge to himself. He said that the Hav-musuvs ruled the sea with fast rowing ships, trading with far-way peoples, and they had flying ships. They were a peaceful people living in the Panamint Mountains of Death Valley near a great lake.

He claimed these strange people had tube-like weapons that could stun a person with a prickly feeling like "a rain of cactus needles." One could not move for hours. The other weapon, a long silvery tube, was deadly and if they pointed it at you, death followed immediately. (The description sounds like a laser).

Oga-Make described the people as having golden tinted skin with their long dark hair held back by a headband. They dressed always in white fine-spun garment that wrapped around them and draped over one shoulder. Sandals were worn on their feet.

An article appeared in the September 1949 issue of FATE magazine, titled, "Tribal Memories of the Flying Saucers." Oddly, the same legend was repeated by an old prospector named Bourke Lee in his book, *Death Valley Men* (Macmillan Co., New York 1932). Lee stated that the story was not legend, but a factual account of the discovery of a now abandoned city within the Panamint Mountains which had been given to him by three men who claimed to have seen this ancient city beneath the desert.

Poverty Point Mound Mystery

In 1966 my great aunt and uncle in West Carroll Parish, Northern Louisiana invited to me visit them. During the month I was taken to civil war battle fields, the City New Orleans, Mississippi, parts of Arkansas, and an ancient site called Poverty Point (Pointe de Pavreté) State heritage site in the northeastern Louisiana. It's a mystery because little is known about these ancient people, also known as mound builders, who employed amazing feats of work between fourteen and eighteen centuries before the birth of Christ. Although this highly advanced race is now extinct, they are known to have been ancestors of Native Americans, such as the Creek, Choctaw, Shawnee, and Natchez.

The site expands within a 25-mile radius of Poverty Point. Archaeologists who excavated part of the tail of the largest bird mound at Poverty Point, rising up 70 feet high and 640 feet along the wing and 710 feet from head to tail, discovered nothing that indicated the purpose of the mound. Excavations have determined the mounds were not used for burial purposes.

What appeared to be an amphitheater was uncover at Poverty Point—a huge geometric layout that suggested the earthworks there involved a master plan in a massive all-out building program. It is not known the true function of the C-shaped plaza, but it is speculated it was a grand ceremonial center. At the time the earthworks were constructed, they were the largest in North America.

Artist's concept of Poverty Point C-shaped plaza estimated 1350 B.C.

It's fascinating that ancient civilizations worldwide built

towering monuments, temples, pyramids and mounds. Did advanced beings teach them that mountains and tall structures pointing to the heavens held great energy or were they honoring the Sky beings from the stars who taught them advanced sciences?

Through the years I have experienced special energies of mountains and their mystical powers. The times I climbed Mount Baldy in South Central Idaho, rising 9,150 feet above the valley floor, I felt a presence of clarity and peace; sounds were richer and the air seemed purer. It's hard to explain, but mountain climbers feel the same exhilaration. I've climbed smaller mountains in central Idaho, and even attempted to climb Mount Borah, Idaho's tallest mountain, standing at 12,668 feet. For me, the climb ended one hour into the three hour climb due to exhaustion and fear of falling. Several climbers have died trying to reach Mount Borah's peak.

Ancient people knew that wherever energy gathered in a mountain vortex was sacred. These highly energetic areas around the globe have been placed where man chose to build megalithic monuments, pyramids, churches, temples and other centers of spiritual learning.

There are three types of energy vortexes:
- Electric—stimulates and energizes
- Magnetic—attracts energy to the area
- Electromagnetic—both activates and attracts

These energy places around the globe are Mother Earth's chakra points. Not only are they places of meditation and healing, but believed to be portals to other realities. It is believed that these portals are keys to past, present and future worlds.

Although some may think vortexes and energy grids are fantasy, science is beginning to prove that this ancient knowledge is fact. In 1973, three Russians—historian Nikolai Goncharov, construction engineer Vyacheslav Morozov, and electronics specialist Valery Makarov, announced in the science journal for the Soviet Academy of Science, Chemistry and Life, their discovery of a geometric grid pattern which appears to interlink a wide number of natural phenomena into a single planetary system. Their work was based on the findings of American researcher and biologist Ivan T. Sanderson (1911-1973), who identified what he called twelve vile vortexes or electromagnetic energy disturbances located equidistant over the surface of the globe, the so-called Bermuda Triangle near the Caribbean and the Devil's Sea off Japan being two of these in his book, *Invisible Residents.*

What the three Russians found was an underlying framework linking these centers into a dual crystal structure, a combination between an icosahedron and a dodecahedron. Not surprisingly, these happen to be the Fourth and Fifth Solids in the Platonic series, which were projected outward by the Earth for over the last million years or so. There is at least one major chakra on each continent. The cardinal seven chakras are:

- 1st chakra - Mt. Shasta, California
- 2nd chakra - Lake Titicaca, South America
- 3rd chakra - Uluru-Katatjuta, Australia
- 4th chakra - Glastonbury-Shaftesbury, England
- 5th chakra - Great Pyramid-Mt. of Olives
- 6th chakra - Kuh-e Malek Siah, Iran
- 7th chakra - Mt. Kailas, Tibet.

There are also four vortexes that govern the four elements. These are spinning energy portals where rituals done in a circle can open and heal the Earth, the participants and people at large. These four vortexes are situated at:

- Earth - Table Mountain and Cape Town, South Africa
- Water - Lake Rotopounamu, North Island, New Zealand
- Air – Egypt's Great Pyramid, Mount of Olives, Jerusalem
- Fire - Haleakala Crater, Hawaii.

Some believe that certain vortexes are negative or vile in energy such as the Bermuda Triangle.

Other locations believed to be energy vortexes are:

- Sedona, Arizona
- Machu Picchu in Peru
- Nazca Plains of Peru
- Tibet
- Sinai desert
- Ayers Rock, Australia
- Mount Fuji volcano, Japan
- Easter Island

Sacred Rocks and Stones

Stones have been invested with sacredness from the earliest times. Stones were worshipped in most ancient cultures, and sacred stones can be found in most of the world's religions. Some were used for divination and others for luck.

Megalithic stone structures can be found throughout the world. Beginning as early as 5,000 BCE, large stones were erected across prehistoric Europe to stand in lines or in circles, like those found at Stonehenge in England. It is believed they mark a sacred place in the landscape. The most remarkable mystery is how these megalithic stones were moved by ancient man.

Crystal skulls have been found throughout Central America and are believed to have mystical qualities and unknown energy. Unfortunately, a great number of the crystal skulls have been removed from their place of origin where they held the balance of the Earth's energy grids.

In 1993, I was invited by a friend to visit Belize in Central America. On our third day, late afternoon, Michael and I drove on the Western Highway to the small village of San Jose Succotz. We found the ferry owner and asked if he'd take across the Mopan River to visit the ancient city of Xunantunich, but he reminded us it was after 5:00 p.m., and that he stopped his ferry crossings at exactly 5 p.m. Unable to change the ferry owner's mind, we swam across the fast-moving river to reach the ancient city.

Xunantunich, eighty miles west of Belize City in the Cayo District, had been an ancient archaeological site that existed during the Classic period and survived the Maya collapse to remain an important population center until approximately 1000 BCE. We reached the site after hiking a mile up a dirt road. Xunantunich means "Stone Woman" in Mayan language. There is a legend that says the "Stone Woman" refers to the ghost of a woman claimed to inhabit the site since 1892. She is always seen dressed completely in white, and has fire-red glowing eyes. She generally appears in front of "El Castillo," ascending the stone stairs, and disappears into a stone wall. There are also stories that the stone woman has been seen emerging from a space craft.

As we climbed up "El Castillo, the main temple, within

minutes we heard dogs barking and soon found yourselves face to face with three Maya men holding machetes. Michael explained in Spanish that we had missed the ferry and swam across the river to see the site. This brought laughter from the men, which calmed our fears. One of the elder men stepped forward and explained in English that he was the caretaker for the site, offering to give us a tour of the Xunantunich ruins.

Author at Altun Ha Maya ruins near Belize City

    As we walked through the courtyard I asked our guide if the Maya had any legends about the stone structures and how they were built. He said, "My people have a legend our ancestors had the ability to make huge stones float in air." I was shocked by his words—the ancient Maya had the technology of levitation. This was the first time I had heard about stones floating in air.

    We thank your guide watching the sun sink lower in the West. Soon we were the pitch black of night, trying to find our way back on the dirt road leading to the river without flashlight or any light to guide our way. We walked quickly, tripping on rocks and slapping the mosquitos and noseeum eating us alive. Reaching the river, we dove in and crossed the swift-moving river, returning to our Jeep.

    The Maya tell of Sky People who came from the heavens in flying ships and taught them astronomy, math and other advanced technologies, and perhaps how to levitate tons of stone. Barbara Marciniak wrote about the Mayan civilization in her book, *Earth: Pleiadian Keys to the Living Library,* and how the Maya were keepers of time, able to anchor on Earth the data that would make sense to future generations, because they were multidimensional. They understood time travel, and could move backward, forward, and sideways in time—their civilization was based on time travel. There are many clues to their technology buried throughout the land of Mexico and Central America.

I can imagine the shamans and Maya leaders looking into the future, and creating their unique calendar, that ended on December 21, 2012. Perhaps the Maya calendar wasn't a prediction of an apocalyptic end for Earth, but a new beginning... or like the Hopi, did their calendar announce a date, a turning point, where humanity can either choose to heal the planet or destroy it?

A small framed man named Edward Leedskalnin, an eccentric Latvian emigrant, may have stumbled on the mysteries of the Great Pyramids and other megalithic stone structures when he started constructing his Coral Castle during the 1920s in Southern Florida. How he was able to quarry, sculpture and move coral rock weighing over 1,100 short tons is still one of the wonders of the world. Leedskalnin died on January 7, 1951 at age 64, taking his knowledge with him. In various documents he wrote about theories of magnetism and in his reply to whoever asked about his method of moving tons of stone, he said, "I understand the laws of weight and leverage and I know the secrets of the people who built the pyramids."

Globally, there are sacred places believed to be time gates and portals where shamans and those who channel higher entities can access these time portals and time corridors. But they must be entered with care and knowledge or many events can blindly trample through what is called time, moving from one place to another like tidal waves pulverizing existence.

There is so much we don't understand about our planet and its relationship to the cosmos and to us. Mother Earth is alive and in her third dimensional existence there exists other world within worlds that we can't see or even comprehend. The fabric of time can be torn apart and chaos can rein, but there are those who know how to ride the corridors and balance worlds and time.

Sound like science fiction? Well, everyday our scientists and physicists are learning more and more about quantum physics and our unseen world. What was fiction yesterday is today's reality.

Uluru (aka Australia's Ayers Rock

    Uluru, also known as Ayers Rock, is located in the Kata Tjuta National Park, a geological wonder and sacred place to the Anangu, the Aboriginal people of the southern part of the northern territory in central Australia. The sandstone formation has a circumference of 5.8 miles and stands 1,142 feet high, rising like a lone island from the stark desert floor, at 2,831 feet above level, with most of it underground. Most geologists believe Ayers rock was the remnants of a vast sedimentary bed laid down some 600 million years ago. Over the eons of time the bed was raised and folded by Earth's crustal movements. Although Ayers Rock is gray underneath, the top part is a distinctive red from the iron oxide coating. Uluru also changes color at different times of the day and year, most notably when it glows red at dawn and sunset. Aboriginal people revere Uluru as sacred.

    According to the Anangu, traditional landowners of Uluru, the world was once a featureless place. None of the places we know existed until creator beings, in the forms of people, plants and animals, traveled widely across the land. Then, in a process of creation and destruction, they formed the landscape as we know it today. Anangu land is still inhabited by the spirits of dozens of these ancestral creator beings which are referred to as *Tjukuritja* or *Waparitja*.

    It is a place of mysticism, a place from where much of their Aboriginal Dreaming emanates. Their mythology of Ayers Rock tells how their ancestor's bodies hardened into rock, and the rock's many caves and fissures are thought to be evidence of this. Some of the forms around Uluru are said to represent ancestral spirits. It was there at the Alcheringa (the Dawn of Time) and will be there until the very end. It holds peace and power.

According to Aboriginal legends, in their mythic beginning when the world was forming known as Alcherina, the Dreamtime, their ancestral beings appeared in the form of totemic animals and humans emerged from the interior of the Earth and began to wander over the land. As the Dreamtime ancestors roamed the Earth they created features of the landscape through their daily lives like birth, death, marriage, hunting, fishing, and singing. At the end of Dreamtime, these features hardened into stone, and the bodies of the ancestors turned into hills, boulders, caves, lakes, and other distinctive landforms.

Human settlement in the Uluru region has been estimated to be more than twenty-two thousand years old. During certain times of the year various Aboriginal tribes would make journeys, called walkabouts, along the songlines of various totemic spirits, returning years after year to the same traditional routes. As they traveled these routes, they sang sacred songs that told the myths of the Dreamtime and gave travel directions across the vast desert to other sacred places along the songlines. Walkabouts conducted along the songlines of their sacred geography were a way to support the spirits of the living Earth, and also a way to preserve their ancient heritage through stories.

Aboriginal legends tell of a time when they came from a distance planet that was dying and ventured to planet Earth as Aboriginal spiritual leader Alinta explained in the first chapter. However, experts believe ancient native Australians migrated from Africa to Asia around 70,000 years ago, and settled in Australia around 50,000 years ago. According to palaeoanthropologist Mike Morwood, of the University of New England in Armidale, his paper confirmed what many experts already believed—"that modern humans first appeared in Africa around 200,000 years ago, and that they dispersed out of Africa."

I believe there is still much more to the history of Earth and its inhabitants. Today, sacred rituals are still held in the caves around the base of Ayers Rock.

Petroglyphs by the Ancients
During the 1990s, I spent ten years in search of ancient

petroglyphs, carved and etched symbols on rock, in Northern Nevada, and discovered evidence of a very ancient Indian culture. Archaeologists from the CSI (College of Southern Idaho) had cataloged and dated pictographs in the area, but they weren't aware of the older petroglyphs until a friend and I discovered them quite by accident.

Pictographs are rock paintings often found in caves and on rock faces and created by Native people depicting hunting scenes, animals and mystical figures or symbols. Normally pictographs are created without any pecking or abrasive methods. In order to create paint for their rock art powdered minerals, blood, charcoal, or other substances were used.

My friend Michael and I spent ten years hiking the remote high desert Nevada area and discovered mysterious rock formations, created by indigenous people of North America. Many of the rock formations actually morphed into animals and humans at different times of the day. A menacing serpent's head sits high on a lava ridge, etched deep into the basalt rock to form the mouth, nose and eye of a serpent. Another rock formation appeared to be the profile of an American Indian with an eye and mouth, and wearing head ornaments. Interestingly, as the shadows fell later in the day that same rock morphed into a coyote.

Each time I visited the area I recited prayers and a blessing, and burned sage to honor the ancestor spirits that still reside there. It's a sacred place, and hopefully it will remain that way without people destroying it with graffiti.

Petroglyph discovered in Northern Nevada. Note: profile of Indian, eye and beaded hair ornament

Who were the ancient people of Northern Nevada who appeared to have worshipped serpents like ancient cultures worldwide? The archaeologists from CSI (College of Southern Idaho) examined the weather-worn petroglyphs, and estimated them to be several thousands of years old, predating the more recent cave pictographs found throughout the area.

What is now the state of Nevada was once home to American Indian people for several millennia prior to the arrival of the first Europeans in America. Today the Great Basin of Nevada is inhospitable high desert, but the area was far different 12,000 years ago when the ice fields began to retreat from North America and by 10,000 BCE Indian people were living in the Black Rock Desert in northwestern Nevada. There is evidence of much more water available and running streams and rivers in Northern Nevada during that time where the people gathered mollusks. Their shells have been uncovered around caves in Northern Nevada.

However, the archaeological data from Nevada is rather scarce and much isn't known about the people who lived there during this time except from their rock art sites with pictograph and petroglyph panels, rockshelters, chipping sites where stone tools were produced, hunting blinds, and open campsites. But as I learned from my excavations in the area, there is still much to be deciphered from these ancient peoples. The petroglyphs of circles, lines and dots still haven't been deciphered, but archaeologist hypothesize it was a form of calendar which included moon cycles and hunting seasons.

I found certain rock placements which might have been related to the summer and winter solstice. But this is only my speculation.

Pictographs found in a Northern Nevada cave

Earth Energy

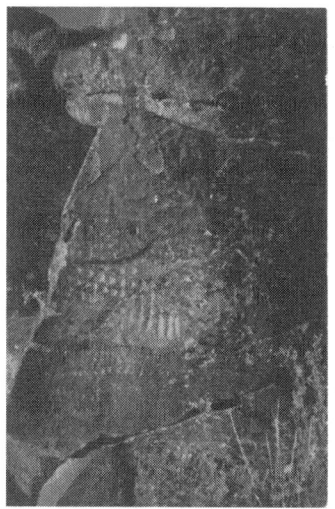

Northern Nevada ancient rock serpent sculpture and petroglyphs

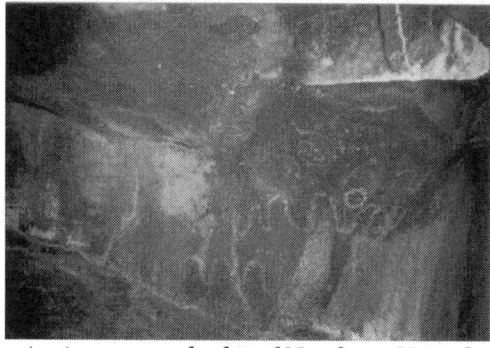

Ancient petroglyphs of Northern Nevada

Prayer for the Land, the water, everything by Western Shoshone Spiritual Leader Corbin Harney

I pray to the Earth to continue to rotate in a clean way.
I talk to the rocks in my prayers. I ask the rocks,
Make sure that you are in such a way that we hear from you.
Make your voices heard; make sure that I hear what you're saying.
Make sure that when we walk on you, we don't stumble on you.
Rocks, I'm asking you to continue to be good to us in all ways, and not to harm us.

"Sometimes I talk for hours to all our plant life. I tell our food to continue to grow. All our food life must have a good life, too."

I pray that you continue to have a good life.
I pray that you have good soil to stand on, and that everything that gives us food is good, and that you go about living your lives just as we do.
I pray that you continue to grow, and have good roots, so that we can feed on you in order to stay healthy, and that the food you make give us the strength we need.

I ask the fire to burn clean, to cook our food in such a way that it won't harm us.

Fire, burn clean.
Burn clean so that we can use you.
You can warm the Mother Earth when you burn, but don't harm anything. Make sure that we, as a people, and the animal life, and the bird life, can use you to heat our bodies, so that way we keep our Mother Earth as clean as can be.
Fire, keep on burning.

Prayer to Mountains by Corbin Harney

I bless the mountain by asking the mountain to bless us:
Mountain, because you're here, sticking out of the ground, it's very important that you take care of our water when it comes from you, from underneath you.
Make sure the water comes out clean from you—so we can use you, pure, clean Water, and so we can drink you and wash with you.

And now I ask you, today, Mountain, to continue to have a voice, to have songs—because through you, we can hear the wind whistle through your rocks.

And your jagged rocks, I'm asking you rocks to be sure to take care of my bird, the Eagle, so that he may land and fly over you in a healthier way, and so he'll feel good flying on top of you.

"This is what I say to the mountain. If the mountain doesn't have a voice, then we as a people are not going to have a voice pretty quick. All the living things are not going to have any voice, because the mountain is where the voice comes from."

Mother Earth provides us with food, provides us with air, and provides us with water. We, the people, are going to have to put our thoughts together, our power together to save our planet here. We've only got one water, one air, one Mother Earth." —Spiritual Leader of the Western Shoshone Native Corbin Harney

CHAPTER FOUR
Fire Element

Gender – Male, Color – Red, Direction South, Season – Summer

Fire is an element of change. It contains magic within itself. Fire is the spark of life in all living things. It is the most spiritual and most physical element of the four elements—water, air, earth and fire. Our planet was formed by the molten lava oozing and sometimes exploding forth from our planet's interior. In the Hawaiian Islands, Pele is the deity or goddess of molten fountains, great lava flows, who reveals herself throughout the Island of Hawaii. Pele is the goddess of fire, lightning, dance, volcanoes and violence. She is also known as *Ka wahine 'ai honua,* the woman who devours the land. She is both creator and destroyer.

According to legends, Pele often appears as a tall, beautiful young woman or a very old, ugly woman. It is said she asks for food or drink and those who are generous and share with her have their lives spared. Those who are greedy are punished by having their homes or crops destroyed.

Pele's most infamous legend is the curse she puts on anyone disturbing or stealing anything from her home land. People who have taken a rock or piece of lava as a souvenir have reported bad luck in their lives. It might be chalked up to silly superstitious nonsense if it wasn't for the thousands of pieces of lava rock mailed back to Hawaii each year by people who claim they met with some horrible misfortune after taking a rock.

In early spring of 1980 my father had a peculiar dream of a beautiful, young woman who spoke to him and said she was the Goddess Pele. My father woke from the dream, sensing Pele, the Hawaiian Goddess of Volcanoes, had actually visited him with urgent message. The dream haunted him for days. During that time I had a dream of a volcano exploding and sensed it was a forewarning a cataclysmic event involving Mount St. Helens volcano which has become extremely active.

My dream and my father's dream of Pele became apparent on May 18, 1980 at 8:32 am PDT. Mount St. Helens, one of the active volcanoes of the Cascade Range in southern Washington, erupted with catastrophic force. Fifty-seven people were killed, 250 homes, 47 bridges, 15 miles of railways and 185 miles of highway were destroyed. A massive debris avalanche triggered by an earthquake measuring 5.1 on the Richter scale caused a massive eruption and pyroclastic flow that reduced the elevation of the mountain's summit from 9,677 feet to 8,365 feet.

Rituals of fire are considered rituals of energy, power, sex, healing, destruction, and cleansing. The discovery of fire, or, more precisely, the controlled use of fire was, of necessity, one of the earliest of human discoveries. Fire's purposes were multiple—light to see in the dark, heat for warmth and to cook, to frighten predators, to clear forests for planting, to heat-treat stone for making stone tools, and to burn clay for ceramic objects.

The earliest evidence for fire use by humans comes from the Oldowan hominid sites in the Lake Turkana region of Kenya, carbon dated to 1.6 million years ago. The site of Chesowanja in central Kenya also contained burned clay clasts, in small areas. Other lower Paleolithic sites in Africa contain evidence for fire in

Ethiopia where burned rock was found and in the Wonderwerk Cave burned ash and bone fragments were found, which date to 1-million years ago.

The earliest evidence of controlled use of fire is found at the Gesher benot Ya'aqov in Israel, where charred wood and seeds were recovered dating 790,000 years ago. However, the next oldest site is at Zhoukoudian, a Lower Paleolithic site in China dated to about 400,000 BP, and at Qesem Cave (Israel), between about 200,000-400,000 years ago.

Eons ago, people considered fire one of the basic elements of the universe, along with water, air and Earth. Like all the elements on Earth, fire can be a source of comfort, heat and light, but it can also be deadly.

The Pima people of the southwestern United States believe that fire appeared in the world to dispose of the dead. In Hindu mythology, Agni, the fire god, represented the essential energy of life in the universe. He consumed life only so that other things can live. Fiery horses pull Agni's chariot as he carried a flaming spear. Agni created the sun and the stars, and his powers were believed great. He made worshippers immortal and purified the souls of the dead from sin. One ancient myth about Agni says that he consumed so many offerings from his worshippers that he became tired. To regain his strength, he had to burn an entire forest with all its inhabitants.

Phoenix Bird

The Phoenix is a mythological bird that is commonly associated with fire or the sun. The story of the Phoenix includes concepts of death and rebirth.

Greek mythology tells of a bird of beautiful plumage that builds a nest and sets itself on fire. From the ashes emerges a new reborn phoenix, associated with the sun. While there are other versions of the story where the phoenix simply dies, decomposes before being reborn again. The symbology of the phoenix death and rebirth is often associated with the concept of reincarnation. In other historical records, the phoenix symbolized renewal of the sun, time, an empire, and resurrection of a heavenly paradise, according to Christian versions of the story.

Some scholars point to the origin of the phoenix or benu bird in ancient Egypt and its association with Heliopolis. The benu was a solar bird that seemed to have a connection to the mythology of the ancient Greek phoenix. Heliopolis "city of the sun" is one of the oldest cities of ancient Egypt. The ancient Egyptian cult center Junu, named "On" in the Hebrew bible, and was renamed Heliopolis by the Greeks in recognition of the sun god, Ra, who presided there.

Chinese Mythology

There are stories of Hui Lu, a magician and fire god who kept 100 firebirds in a gourd. By setting them loose, he could start a fire across the whole country. There was also a hierarchy of gods in charge of fire. At its head was Lo Hsüan, whose cloak, hair, and beard were red. Flames spurted from his horse's nostrils. He was not unconquerable, however. Once when he attacked a city with swords of fire, a princess appeared in the sky and quenched his flames with her cloak of mist and dew.

The bringers of fire are legendary heroes in many traditions. Prometheus of Greek mythology, one of the most famous fire bringers, stole fire from the gods and gave it to humans. Similar figures appear in the tales of other cultures.

Native Americans believe that long ago some evil being hid fire so that people could not benefit from it. A hero had to recover it and make it available to human beings. In many versions of the story, Coyote steals fire for people, but sometimes a wolf, woodpecker, or other animal has that ability to do so. According to the Navajo, Coyote tricked two monsters that guarded the flames on Fire Mountain. Then he lit a bundle of sticks tied to his tail and ran down the mountain to deliver the fire to his people.

African traditions also say that animals gave fire to humans. The San of South Africa believe that Ostrich guarded fire under his wing until a praying mantis stole it. Mantis tricked Ostrich into spreading his wings and made off with the fire. The fire destroyed Mantis, but from the ashes came two new Mantises.

The Indians of the Amazon River basin in Brazil say that a jaguar rescued a boy and took him to its cave. There the boy watched the jaguar cooking food over a fire. The boy stole a hot coal from the fire and took it to his people, who then learned how to cook.

Legends in the Caroline Islands of the Pacific link fire to Olofat, a mythical trickster hero who was the son of the sky god and a mortal woman. As a youth, Olofat forced his way into heaven to see his father. Later Olofat gave fire to human beings by allowing a bird to fly down to earth with fire in its beak.

A Crow sweat lodge.--Museum of the American Indian

Native American Sweat Lodge Fire Pit
Humans have always been obsessed with fire. And through the ages humans continued to experiment with fire, creating electricity and finally destructive atomic and nuclear explosions, the ultimate and most deadly human-made fire.

The American Indian sweat lodge ceremony is not ancient. It was an adaptation of the sweat bath common to many ethnic cultures found in North and South America, Asia, Eastern and Western Europe, and Africa. It sprang from European culture when native people felt they were corrupting them and their culture. With the introduction of alcohol and the inhumane treatment of native people, the need to re-purify themselves and find their way back to traditional ways of living became evident, as they were becoming increasingly poisoned by European culture. The sweat lodge with the help of medicine men and women became a place where they could heal their spirits, their minds and their bodies. It was also a place where they could communicate to spirits, their ancestors, totem helpers, Creator and Mother Earth/four directions for needed wisdom and power.

Sweat Lodge Prayer
Grandfather, Mysterious One,
We search for you along this
Great Red Road you have set us on.
Sky Father, Tunkashila,
We thank you for this world.
We thank you for our own existence.
We ask only for your blessing and for your instruction.
Grandfather, Sacred One,
Put our feet on the holy path that leads to you,
and give us the strength and the will
to lead ourselves and our children
past the darkness we have entered.
Teach us to heal ourselves,
to heal each other and to heal the world.
Let us begin this very day,
this very hour,
the Great Healing to come.
Let us walk the Red Road in Peace.

Lightning and Sprites
From time to time I've had psychic experiences and premonitions during electrical storms. How or why this happens is unknown to me. One explanation is that lightning contains both negative and positive charged ions. Lightning is caused by the separation of electrical charges within a cloud. The electrical charges are carried by ions—atoms or groups of atoms that have either gained electrons, making them negatively charged, or lost electrons, making them positively charged.

Lightning still holds many mysteries for scientists. One such mystery is the phenomenon of sprites, large-scale electrical discharges that occur high above thunderstorm clouds giving rise to a quite varied range of visual shapes flickering in the night sky. Luminous reddish-orange sprites have been seen and captured on video by astronauts on ISS (International Space Station) orbiting Earth. They are triggered by the discharges of positive lightning between an underlying thundercloud and the ground. Perhaps the best way to describe them is more like a fluorescent tube discharge than lightning discharges at an altitude of 31 to 56 miles above Earth's surface.

Another enigma of lightning is known as "ball lightning." Ball lightning is an unexplained atmospheric electrical phenomenon. The term refers to reports of luminous, spherical-shaped objects that vary from marble-sized to several meters. They are usually associated with thunderstorms, and last longer than a flash of lightning. Through the years there have been stories of fatalities linked to ball lightning, but these are only stories. Scientists have proposed theories about ball lightning over the centuries, but so far the true nature of ball lightning is still unknown.

During my high school years in southern Idaho, a friend reported that her brothers had a terrifying experience in the middle of the night during a thunderstorm. A glowing ball of light shot through their bedroom window, danced around the room and then shot back out the window. Luckily, they were unharmed.

Aurora Borealis

An aurora is a natural light display in the sky taken from the Latin word *aurora*, "sunrise" or the Roman goddess of dawn. The aurora borealis (the Northern Lights) and the aurora australis (the Southern Lights) have always fascinated mankind, and people even travel thousands of miles just to see a brilliant light show in the Earth's atmosphere. The auroras, both surrounding the north magnetic pole (aurora borealis) and south magnetic pole (aurora australis) occur when highly charged electrons from the solar wind interact with elements in the Earth's atmosphere. Solar winds stream away from the sun at speeds of about 1 million miles per hour. When they reach the earth, some 40 hours after leaving the sun, they follow the lines of magnetic force generated by the Earth's core and flow through the magnetosphere, a teardrop-shaped area of highly charged electrical and magnetic fields.

As electrons enter Earth's upper atmosphere, they encounter atoms of oxygen and nitrogen at altitudes from 20 to 200 miles above the Earth's surface. The color of the aurora depends on which atom is struck, and the altitude of the meeting. Most auroras or Northern Lights can be white ribbons dancing across the sky, but sometimes brilliant red, green, yellow, pink and blue are seen. The atomic oxygen and ionized molecular nitrogen is responsible for the color variations.

The first time I witnessed an aurora borealis was on my way to Calgary, Alberta Canada. A white ribbon of light undulated across the sky like a snake. My second aurora sighting was over Tucson, Arizona. Unknown to me at the time, a major solar flare had erupted from the sun on March 29, 2001, that caused a geomagnetic storm to hit Earth's atmosphere the following night, Friday, March 30, 2001. It was around 11:30 p.m. Mountain Time, I heard Art Bell on Coast to Coast AM radio announce the sighting of Northern Lights north of his Pahrump, Nevada home. I ran outside and stood in awe of the blood-red glow in the northern sky, coming slightly from the east. The aurora had fingers or beams of light coming from it. What made this so unusual is the aurora borealis is seldom seen this far south of the Arctic. I still wonder if the eerie blood-red aurora that night was a supernatural warning about the tragic events of September 11, 2001, the morning planes operated by terrorists brought down the World Trade Center buildings in New York City.

There are many legends and folklore about the aurora borealis which has intrigued people from ancient times, and still does today. The Eskimos and Indians of North America have many stories to explain the northern lights.

The Point Barrow Eskimos were the only Eskimo group who considered the aurora an evil omen. In the past they carried knives to keep it away from them. The Fox Indians, who lived in Wisconsin, regarded the light as an omen of war and pestilence. To them the lights were the ghosts of their slain enemies who, restless for revenge, tried to rise up again. Most Eskimo groups have a myth of the northern lights as the spirits of the dead playing ball with a walrus head or skull. The Eskimos of Nunivak Island had the opposite idea, of walrus spirits playing with a human skull. The east Greenland Eskimos thought that the northern lights were the spirits of children who died at birth. The dancing of the children round and round caused the continually moving streamers and draperies of the aurora. The Makah Indians of Washington State thought the lights were fires in the Far North, over which a tribe of dwarfs, half the length of a canoe paddle, and so strong they caught whales with their hands. An Algonquin myth tells of when Nanahbozho, creator of the Earth, had finished his task of the creation, he traveled to the north, where he remained. He built large fires, of which the northern lights are the reflections, to remind his people that he still thinks of them.

One of the strangest aurora borealis stories took place in 1927. Lucia dos Santos, cloistered Carmelite nun, was instructed by Jesus to reveal the secret given to her and her two cousins during one of the Blessed Virgin Mary visitations in Fatima, Portugal in 1917. The Lady had warned of five scourges to transpire and the first one give was: "When you shall see the night illuminated by an unknown light, know that it is a great sign that God is giving you that He is going to punish the world for its crimes by means of war."

That sign, as prophesied, came on the night of January 25, 1938, when all of Europe and part of North America were lighted by an extraordinarily brilliant display of the aurora borealis. Lucia, peering at the amazing light show from her convent cell, recognized it as the promised warning of war to come. World War II began in 1939. The skies over Europe were so brilliant red that Londoners believed their entire city was aflame.

Light Spirit, our Star—Grandfather Sun

Our world is unique with only one star in our solar system—the sun. Our Sun lies at the heart of our solar system, but it still holds many secrets. The miracle of the sun is that it's not too big or too close to fry Earth. The Sun is a pretty small star compared to the giants in the Universe. Only about one out of one hundred stars are more than eight times as massive as our Sun. The largest star, Mu Cepheim is so large you could fit over one billion of our Suns inside of it! Most stars are less massive than the Sun. The smallest are only about three times as big as Earth and about one out of ten stars are similar in mass to our Sun.

Without the Sun's intense energy and heat, there would be no life on Earth. And although it is special to us, there are billions of stars like our sun scattered across the Milky Way Galaxy.

Theories abound that once our solar system had a binary star, but it became a brown dwarf or failed star, known today as Planet X or Nibiru. Although Nibiru has never been officially found, legends persist, including those who believe that increased Earth changes and extreme weather patterns are the result of Planet X passing through our solar system at this time.

Zecharia Sitchin was an author who proposed an explanation for human origins involving ancient astronauts. He believed a race of extraterrestrials from the planet Nibiru, Planet X, influenced the ancient Sumerian people. The scenario outlined in Sitchin's book, *The Twelfth Planet,* and its sequels, stated Nibiru returned to the inner solar system every 3,600 years.

In the last two years, astronomers discovered several exoplanets in binary systems: two stars locked in mutual orbit. These systems come in several types, with the planet orbiting one or both stars. About half the binary systems involve stars that are very far apart: 1000 times the Earth-Sun separation or more. Whether or not Planet X exists is still to be determined.

The sun, a star, changes the dark of night into light, warms our bodies, and brings forth life to all things. The dynamics of our sun are miraculous, and the greater miracle is how Earth came to possess life when all other planets in our planet are devoid of it.

Our sun is at the center of our Solar System. It is almost perfectly spherical and consists of hot plasma interwoven with magnetic fields. It has a diameter of about 1,392,684 km or 865,374 miles, approximately 109 times that of Earth and its mass is approximately 330,000 times the mass of Earth which accounts for about 99.86% of the total mass of the Solar System. It is made up of mostly hydrogen while the rest is helium. Scientists believe the sun formed around 4.567 billion years ago from the gravitational collapse of a region with a large molecular cloud.

Should we worry that someday the Sun will go supernova? It does not have enough mass to explode as a supernova, but in approximately 5 billion years or so, it will grow steadily brighter as more helium accumulates in its core. As the supply of hydrogen dwindles, the Sun's core must keep producing enough pressure to keep the Sun from collapsing in on itself. The only way it can do this is to increase its temperature. Eventually it will run out of hydrogen fuel. At that point, it will go through a radical change which will most likely result in the complete destruction of the planet Earth. It is calculated that the Sun will become large enough to engulf the current orbits of the solar system's inner planets, and maybe even Earth. Before it does become a red giant, the luminosity of the Sun will have doubled, and the Earth will be hotter than Venus is today. Once the core hydrogen is exhausted in 5.4 billion years, the Sun will expand into its subgiant phase and slowly double in size over about half a billion years. It will then expand more rapidly over about half a billion years until it is over two hundred times larger than today and a couple of thousand times more luminous. This then starts the red giant branch (RGB) phase where the Sun will spend approximately a billion years and lose around a third of its mass.

Our sun is unique for several reasons:
1) Our sun is a solitary star. Whereas many if not most stars are grouped together as binaries, triplets or in clusters.
2) Our sun is a G type star. This is quite a large star compared with the average. Most stars are red dwarfs. It is estimated 9 out of 10 are dwarf stars but this may not be an accurate estimate.
3) Our solar system has existed in the same configuration that we see now for over 4 plus billion years. It is unknown how many stars and their system of planets can continue stability for this long.
4) Our sun exists at the right distance from the galactic center that enables it to rotate around the galaxy at the same rate as the spiral arms. Most stars do not.

Our Sun has inspired mythology in almost every culture; ancient Egyptians, Aztecs of Mexico, the Inca and Maya of South America, North American Indians, and Chinese. In Egyptian mythology, the solar deity or sun goddess was a sky deity who represented the Sun, or an aspect of it, usually by its perceived power and strength. Solar deities and sun worship can be found throughout most of recorded history in various forms. Today, religions like Hinduism still regard the Sun as a God.

There are ancient monuments worldwide that were constructed with the solar deity in mind such as stone megaliths that mark the summer or winter solstice. Some of the most well-known megaliths are found in Nabta Playa, Egypt, Mnajdra in Malta, Ireland, Chichén Itzá, Mexico and Stonehenge, England. The Chichén Itzá monument was designed to cast shadows in the shape of serpents climbing the pyramid at the vernal and autumn equinoxes.

Missing Sun

The missing sun is a theme throughout many cultures. The missing sun is often used to explain various natural phenomena, including the disappearance of the sun at night, shorter days during the winter, and solar eclipses. For those who subscribe to the polar shift theory, it is believed our planet's poles have shifted several times and the sun actually rose in the west and set in the east.

Islam prophesies state that the sun will rise from the West one day, instead of rising from the East, during the End Times, before the Day of Judgment. Both the Quran and the Hadith affirm that this phenomenon will take place. The occurrence of this phenomenon is considered in Islam as one of the major signs that indicate the Day of Judgment is close.

The Sun Dance

The Sun Dance is a ceremony practiced by indigenous peoples of North America and Canada, mostly the Great Plains Indians. There was a dark time for the people when Canada and the United States banned ceremonies, and even outlawed indigenous people from conducting their sacred Sun Dance. It was banned in the latter part of the nineteenth century, partly because certain tribes inflicted self-torture (self-piercing) as part of the ceremony, which settlers found gruesome, and partially as part of a grand attempt to westernize Indians by forbidding them to engage in their ceremonies and speak their language. Those that continued to practice their culture were either imprisoned or killed. Tribes then held ceremonies underground and were practiced in secret.

My spiritual teacher Ed McGaa "Eagle Man" has danced in the Sioux Sun Dance six times in his lifetime. The Sun Dance is a tribal gathering, a tribal beseechment and an expression of thanksgiving. The Sioux Sun Dance Ceremony lasts four days. In times gone by, it was held after the summer buffalo hunts, when the buffalo meat was cured and dried for winter provisions. It was a time of celebration and plenty. The Sun Dance of today is usually held in late July or early August. It is started on a Thursday in order that the fourth day will be a Sunday, a day that most people don't work, says Ed.

Great preparation goes into the Lakota Sioux ceremony where

a large ceremonial tipi is raised, sweat lodges built. On the day before the first ceremony day, a feeling party goes out to a cottonwood tree, and a woman, representative of the Buffalo Calf Woman, takes the first cut on the tree with an axe. She speaks to the tree and tells it that her people are sorry to have to take the tree's life but the ceremony is necessary because it will be the *Wiwanyag Wachipi*, a ceremony in which the people dance, gazing at the sun. It is a ceremony, she explains "highly important, for by doing it, the people will live."

Before the cottonwood tree is planted in the center of the area, a peace pipe is placed in a hole dug for the tree trunk. Cloth banners in the colors of the four directions are tied to the branches with green and blue banners for Mother Earth and Father Sky. That evening a Sweat Lodge ceremony is held for the Sun Dance pledgers. One of the pledges is to promise to undergo the piercing pain of the Sun Dance ceremony. Those who pledge usually take their vow the preceding year and live their lives accordingly, keeping in mind that they will be dancing the ceremony before the people, the spirit world, and ultimately before the six powers of the Universe and *Wakan Tanka*—Great Spirit.

The Sundance is one of our most sacred ceremonies handed down to the Lakota people by the Creator.

The Ancient Egyptians and Ra

The Egyptians worshipped the sun as Ra, as being carried across the sky in a solar barque, accompanied by lesser gods, and to the Greeks the sun was Helios, a god carried in a chariot drawn by fiery horses.

One of my favorite and mysterious Egyptian pharaohs was Akhenaton, ruler of the Eighteenth dynasty of Egypt, who ruled 17 years and died in 1336 B.C. or 1334 B.C. He was radical for his time and is noted for abandoning traditional Egyptian polytheism and introducing worship of Aten, a one god in the form of the sun. He wrote beautiful poems to honor the sun and all living creatures.

Bright is the earth when thou risest in the horizon.
When thou shinest as Aton by day
Thou drivest away the darkness
When thou sendest forth they rays,

*The two lands (Egypt) are in daily festivity,
Awake and standing upon their feet
When thou hast raised them up.
Their limbs bathed, they take their clothing,
Their arms uplifted in adoration in thy dawning.
Then in all the world they do their work.*

Prayer to the Sun by Corbin Harney
*Sun, continue to shine on us, to shine on the Mother Earth here, And make a good reflection on us, so that you will shine in a way that warms the Mother Earth.
Continue to shine on Mother Earth, on all the animals, the birds, the fish, and the human race, on all the flowers, and on all our food, so that they all continue to grow. I pray for the sun and the wind.*

The man who sat on the ground in his tipi meditating on life and its meaning accepting the kinship of all creatures and acknowledging unity with the universe of thing was infusing into his being the true essence of civilization. And when native man left off this form of development, his humanization was retarded in growth. —Oglala Lakota Chief Luther Standing Bear (1868 – 1939)

CHAPTER FIVE
Air Element

Gender – Male, Color – Yellow, Direction – East, Season – Spring

Our planet Earth is blessed to have air or oxygen to sustain life. No other planet in our solar system has enough oxygen to support life as we know it here. Oxygen is a chemical element with symbol O and atomic number 8. By mass, oxygen is the third-most abundant element in the universe, after hydrogen and helium. Air is life!

The air element resides in each of us. As soon as we call to mind the air element within the body—the air in our lungs and other body cavities, even the gases dissolved in our blood—we're immediately aware of the breathing, aware that air is flowing rhythmically in and out of the body. It is the first breath we take at birth.

So almost simultaneously we recall the Air element outside of us—the air surrounding us and touching the skin in this very moment, the winds and clouds and breezes that we see and hear moving tree branches, grasses and flowers.

There's no boundary between inner Air and outer Air. There is only one Air Element, and what's within us is simply borrowed for a few moments. In fact we can only live by letting go, never by holding on. Having this direct sense of interconnectedness with air and all the elements is enlivening and empowering. I've often set beside a river, watched the clouds, felt the wind on my face, knowing I am no longer separate from the elements; I am but an intimate part of the vast cycle of all Earth's spirit elements.

The first peoples of North America considered the wind to be a living force in and of itself. The wind honored in the Four Directions, like a god with power that is capable of communicating a larger-than-life language to those who would hear it. Only a few gifted shaman, medicine men and spiritual leaders among tribe were able to interpret the cosmic messages in nature.

The Inuit Indians had an Air Spirit among the ranks of their Sila (a term that means Wisdom and Weather). Their Air Spirit controlled the seas, skies and wind. Although considered a kind and benevolent spirit, it could strike wrath against liars, beggars and thieves in the form of illnesses. It is also blamed for bad weather and poor hunting.

The Micmac, a tribe belonging to the Wabanaki Confederacy native to New Brunswick and Nova Scotia, migrated to Maine in the United States. There is a story of a hero named Strong Wind who turned evil people (specifically the nefarious sisters of his beloved) into aspen trees, and to this day he makes them tremble in fear when he comes near the aspen forest. According to this legend this is why aspen leaves always shake in the wind. Outside of the United States, the Aztec believed in a wind-god, Ehecatle, who blew the moon and sun into orbit.

From an indigenous perspective, the wind seemed to be personified as divine messenger, able to manipulate unseen energy. What an amazing experience to hear the voice of God emptied into the wind or view the force of the winds and knows it is the soul of a Creator that is sweeping through the land.

The times I spent in the Sawtooth Mountains of Idaho, I listened to the wind rustle the silvered aspen leaves on a fall day and it was magical. I loved the days I sat silently on a rock beside

Dierkes Lake and watched the water ripple from a gentle breeze or a red-tailed hawk flying high above the canyon rim.

During my teen years I was shown the true fierceness of the wind while boating on the 86,000 acre American Falls reservoir near Pocatello, Idaho with friends. It was a hot summer day and several young guys invited my friend Shirley and me on their small boat. Meanwhile, black clouds gathered in the West, building and moving toward us. We didn't think much of it at the time until we were far from shore when the outboard motor stalled as the wind picked up with gusts of fifty-miles an hour as our small boat took on water—fast! We had only a small coffee can to bail out the water and one oar. Huge white water waves grew higher and more threatening as I flashed on the headlines: *Four Teens drown in reservoir.*

My prayers were answered one frightening hour later when our boat was pushed into a cove on the opposite shore from our cars. American Falls reservoir is huge and nearly 50 feet deep, and through the years a great number of people have lost their lives there. We made it to shore, soaked and cold, but I learned a valuable lesson that day about the elements—wind and water can be gentle one minutes, and fierce the next minute. Wind should always be honored and never taken lightly (no pun intended).

Without wind there would be no clouds, no waves on the oceans, and no gentle breezes to cool us in the summer. Without the wind you'd never smell flower in bloom on a spring day or the sagebrush after a rainstorm, you'd never fly a kite high into the sky, or feel the silky breeze caress you skin on a tropical island— there's so much more, but these are the things I love about the wind. There are horrible things that wind can produce like hurricanes, typhoons, and tornadoes, but it's all part of Mother Earth's personality—her beauty, her gentleness, her ferocity, her anger, and her whispers of love carried in the wind.

Mysterious Force Protecting Earth

In an article by Gregg Prescott, M.S. in Waking Times magazine, he cited NASA's recent discovery of what appears to be a "force field" over Earth, fueling the fire over whether our planet has been under spiritual and physical quarantine as many have suggested.

According to Daniel Baker, director of the Laboratory for Atmospheric and Space Physics, the electron barrier exists in the Van Allen belts, a pair of donut-shaped belts that ring the Earth teeming with protons and electrons. The Earth's magnetic field holds the belts in place, but the scientist says that the electrons in these belts which travel at nearly the speed of light are being blocked by some invisible force that reminded him of the kind of shields used in television series like Star Trek to stop alien energy weapons from vaporizing starships.

A number of philosophers and spiritual teachers have speculated that there have been no moon landings due a combination of quarantine and the radiation found in the Allen Belt. Is it protection or a form of quarantine?

Michael Tsarion writes about the quarantine and its association to the moon in the *Stargate and Quarantine* chapter of his book, *Atlantis, Alien Visitation and Genetic Manipulation:* "When the original pursuers of the "Serpent Brotherhood" destroyed the planet Tiamat, they made ready to leave this solar system and return to their own. They had to leave in a hurry, so as not to be hindered by the cosmic forces which would be unleashed throughout the solar system. Because of their haste, they did not have time to precisely scan the planet Earth, and so they did not locate their enemies hidden deep within the caverns and beneath the seas of pre-diluvian Earth. The masters of the Nephilim were relatively convinced that even if their enemies were on Earth they could not survive the paroxysms and furor that Tiamat's obliteration would bring on. However, these unknown pursuers did not just leave our solar system without instigating precautionary measures. Before they made the journey back to their own planet, they established an etheric barrier around our planet that would be along the same orbit trajectory as the Moon's around the Earth. This barrier still exists and is utterly impenetrable to the Atlantean progeny, because the technology by which it was erected was of an extremely advanced level. From that time onwards, the Moon would come to represent (in almost all cultures) arcane powers of protection and magic.

This apotropaic barrier, often referred to as by native peoples as the "the great web in the sky," was put there obviously to prevent the Atlanteans from ever leaving this place. The Earth was to be their tomb."

Grandmother Moon

The Native Americans call her Grandmother Moon. In Roman mythology, she was referred to as Diana, the goddess of the hunt and birth, being associated with wild animals. She had the power to talk to and control animals.

The moon, or Luna in Latin, shines her silver light on Earth at night. The moon is Earth's only natural satellite, although not the largest natural satellite in our Solar System. Its bright white light comes from the sun's light on its gray, crater-marked surface, and it is believed it formed nearly 4.5 billion years ago, about the time of Earth's formation. Scientists have hypothesized that our satellite formed from the debris left over after a giant impact between Earth and a Mars-sized object.

The Moon's gravitational influence produces ocean tides, affects Earth's weather, and may affect human emotion and create large earthquakes. The Moon's current orbital distance is about thirty times the diameter of Earth, causing it to have an apparent size in the sky almost the same as that of the Sun. This allows the Moon to cover the Sun nearly precisely in total solar eclipse. The Moon's linear distance from Earth is currently increasing at 1.504 ± 0.028 inches per year.

As Earth is the Mother of life, Moon is our Grandmother. Without the Moon, there would be no life on Earth. The satellite that orbits our planet has much to do with our weather, ocean cycles, the cycles for all creatures and sea creatures, the cycles in humans and woman's monthly cycle.

Without the Moon to draw the four tides around Earth, only the sun would exert its gravitational influence. It is theorized that the Sun would evaporate moisture into a huge cloud that would always between the Earth and the Sun's light. Earth would get little sunlight. Without the lunar tides, there probably wouldn't be any tectonic activity to create mountains and deep underwater crevasses, so the ocean might be only a kilometer deep all over the planet.

The overall effect would be days of clouded, freezing cold nights, and cold nights. There would be little air, and plant life couldn't exist without access to sunlight, and without the plants, animals would not exist. Without this perfect relationship, our planet wouldn't be protected from the full effects of the sun's heat in the daytime, or the extreme cold of space at night. Without Grandmother Moon we can only imagine what her absence would do to all of biology and reproduction on Earth.

The ancients knew the Moon was the symbol of life itself, and one of the reasons for their existence. Shamans and medicine people planted crops during certain phases of the moon—they recognized the relationship between plants and the Moon's energy. The Moon was celebrated and honored as the source of fertility and growth. The ancient people understood the mysteries of the Moon, but have been given little credit for their wisdom. I have no doubt that Grandmother Moon was responsible for bringing life to our planet and to us. Grandmother moon should be called the mandala of life!

Wind Prayer

O Great Spirit Who's voice I hear in the winds and whose breath gives life to the entire world, hear me! I am small and weak and I need your strength and wisdom.

Let Me Walk in Beauty and make my eyes ever behold the red and purple sunset. Make My Hands respect the things you have made and my ears sharp to hear your voice, Make Me Wise so that I may understand the things you have taught my people; Let Me Learn the lessons you have hidden in every leaf and rock I seek Strength, not to be greater than my brother, but to fight my greatest enemy—Myself. Make Me Always Ready to come to you with clean hands and straight eyes, so When Life Fades, as the fading sunset, my spirit may come to you without shame. Aho! — Author Unknown

Wind Prayer by Corbin Harney

Wind, continue to have a breeze, so that we have clean air to breathe. Continue to move everything, move everything here on the Mother Earth, so that you continue to give us fresh air.

*And Sun, if there is a problem, a bad thing, make the breeze to
blow that away from us, so that way we can have cleaner air.*

Lakota Prayer by Medicine Grizzly Bear
*O Great Creator,
I come before you in a humble manner
and offer you this sacred pipe.
With tears in my eyes and an ancient song from my heart
I pray.
To the four powers of Creation,
To the Grandfather Sun,
To the Grandmother Moon,
To the Mother Earth,
And to my ancestors.
I pray for all my relations in Nature,
All those who walk, crawl, fly and swim,
Seen and unseen,
To the good spirits that exist in every part of Creation.
I ask that you bless our elders and children,
families and friends,
And the brothers and sisters who are in prison.
I pray for the ones who are sick on drugs and alcohol
And for those who are now homeless and forlorn.
I also pray for peace among the four races of humankind.
May there be good health and healing on this earth,
May there be Beauty above me,
May there be Beauty below me,
May there be Beauty in me,
May there be Beauty all around me.
I ask that this world be filled with Peace, Love and Beauty.*

The Forest is life. The Forest is our God-given pharmacy.
—Grandmother Bernadette Rebionot of Africa

CHAPTER SIX
Plant Spirits

How could life on Earth have become so diversified and evolved into an endless number of species? It's a question that certainly leaves me awestruck. Estimates suggest that 100 million species of life exist on our planet, and according to the last forest inventory, almost 247 billion trees over 1 inch in diameter exist in the United States.

During my childhood we lived next to a row of large cottonwood trees, at least one hundred years old. I climbed the trees, and often fantasized I could fly like a bird. Sometimes I escaped to my favorite tree, the largest of the cottonwood trees and hide there, away from my troubled home life. I felt safe within the embrace of the tree's huge branches, away from the harshness of life. I felt the tree's life and energy, and sensed it had a soul.

Ancient people also believed trees had souls and treated them as animate beings that were to be respected and honored. In stories handed down by the Norse, the All Father was said to have created the tree of the universe called *Yggdrasil*, symbolizing all life. For the Greeks, trees were worshipped as Gods. In one legend Zeus inhabited an oak tree, which became known as the "oracular oak."

The Cherokees, Lakota and other American Indian tribes considered trees holy and sacred. They preferred to use trees that had already fallen instead of cutting down living trees. If a tree had to be cut, the people asked permission of the tree, and gifts were offered for its life.

In Denise Linn's book, *Sacred Space,* she writes about the mighty oak tree being sacred to the Celts. The spiritual advisors of the Celtic people were called Druids, meaning "men of the oak trees." Druids communicated using a secret alphabet of twenty-five letters. Fourteen of the letters were named after trees. Each tree expressed a particular spiritual quality that was conveyed through the alphabet letter named after it.

Myths tell of dryads, the spirits of the trees, leaving their tree homes to go into battle in defense of the Celts. The Spirit of the Tree could leave its body, but only for short periods of time, and it could not go very far away from its tree or death would follow. It is said these heroic tree spirits often stayed too long in the battles to help Celtic and died saving their friends.

Trees are also believed to serve as doorways to other worlds for shamans. The tree, in its wisdom, allows the shaman to transition to other worlds and realities. Certain tribes in California used tree stumps to embark on their sacred journeys. The Arunt of Australia use hollow trees to take spiritual journeys and indigenous tribes of the Amazon follow the roots of the tree into the underworlds.

The remarkable thing about trees, a single tree produces approximately 260 pounds of oxygen per year. Two mature trees can supply enough oxygen annually to support a family of four! One tree can absorb as much carbon in a year as a car produces while driving 26,000 miles. It's as if trees were tailor-made for humans and all life to exist and thrive and that's a miracle. The tallest tree in the country is a redwood tree growing in northern California's Redwood National Park which stands at 369 feet tall and is over 2,000 years old!

As a child my parents took my younger sister Kathy and me to visit California's mighty giants—the redwood trees. My first reaction was to run to a giant redwood and attempt to wrap my little arms around it. It made a lasting impression on me. In 1997, I discovered the story of a young environmentalist named Julia Butterfly Hill who climbed a 200-foot redwood in December and stayed there for 738 days to save the tree, dubbed *Luna*, from loggers ready to cut down the thousand-year-old tree. On December 18, 1999, Julia Butterfly Hill's feet touched the ground for the first time in over two years, as she descended from *Luna*, a thousand year-old redwood in Humboldt County, California.

Hill believed she would only be there for a two-to-three week long "tree-sit." The action was meant to stop Pacific Lumber, a division of the Maxxam Corporation, from the environmentally destructive process of clear-cutting the ancient redwood and the trees near it. The area immediately next to Luna had already been stripped and, because of that action, many believed there was nothing left to hold the soil to the mountain, a huge part of the hill from sliding into the town of Stafford.

Described in her book, *The Legacy of Luna,* Hill lived on a makeshift platform eighteen stories off the ground, enduring torrential storms, harassment from angry loggers, extreme cold, El-Nino storms, hurricane-force winds, helicopter harassment, and a ten-day siege by company security guards. But in her loneliness and doubt, she prayed to the Universal Spirit, to *Luna* and heard the tree's voice speak to hear, teaching her to let go, to go with the flow.

Celebrities like Joan Baez, Bonnie Raitt, and Woody Harrelson visited the tree and Julia. Today, Hill continues her environmental activism. Sadly, only 3% of America's majestic ancient redwood forests remain. Now an even more disturbing problem has emerged as poachers enter California's national parks to removed large portions of the redwoods. In Northern California redwood trees are being poached like the lawlessness taking place in the Amazon jungle. Thieves are cutting massive chunks from the base of the ancient trees, which are the tallest on Earth and are up to 2,000 years old. While state officials say the damage is far from any Amazonian deforestation, they do rank the desecration alongside elephant tusk poaching.

Although the trees can live when cut into, an open wound can cause pests and diseases to enter the trees and kill it, and it also becomes destabilized in large windstorms. These giants and all trees provide oxygen and remove pollutants in Earth's air and now they are being destroyed at an alarming rate. Insanity!

Grandmother Agnes Baker Pilgrim of Oregon says, "Life is very precious. Every blade of grass is our relative. Everyone one-legged—the Tree People—needs our voice. The animal kingdom and the swimmers in the water need our voice. They are crying out for help."

Grandmother Agnes also explained in *Grandmothers Counsel the World*, that in a single tree, there are four or five ecosystems, yet on the highways around the world, mighty trees are chained together onto log trucks, ancient giants heading for chipping mills, many to be shipped to Japan, where they are transformed into cardboard boxes to hold stereos, televisions, and other electronic equipment for eager consumers.

Grandmother Agnes has noted the harm clear-cut logging has done when the trees are no longer there to hold the moisture in the soil for the little shoots to grow. The elders of her community believe that if you take the trees off the top of the mountains, you change the climate, because the ancient trees are the ones that call the wind and the rain. "Wind patterns are being destroyed; things that used to grow to hold the ground are being pulled up. Paving has caused erosion all over the lands."

In 1994 I attended a pow wow ceremony in Kamiah, Idaho with the Nez Perce tribe, a gracious and kind people. One of the elders explained to me how clear-cutting of their sacred mountains had changed the weather in that region. Now they receive less rainfall each year.

Through my travels I discovered that children have not been taught how to respect nature. Although I did not witness the event at a local park, several trees had been stripped of their bark, perhaps by teens or children. Hopefully, these children didn't realize the damage they had inflicted on the tree by removing its protective skin. When trees lose their bark there are susceptible to insects, disease and the elements. I pray that parents and school teachers will teach their children how valuable trees are to the world and our very survival.

Today valuable trees found in rainforests throughout the world are being clear cut for planting crops and making room for a growing population. During my first visit to Belize in Central America I was moved to tears where huge areas of forests were being cut and burned to plant orange groves and bananas crops. Environmentalists claim they are killing the natural habitats of indigenous animals and contributing to climate change. Clearcutting has caused the loss of topsoil. A study from the University of Oregon found that in certain zones, areas that were clear cut had nearly three times the amount of erosion and slides. Demand for wood and arable land through clear cutting has led to the loss of over half of the world's rainforests.

The world's rain forests could completely vanish in a hundred years at the current rate of deforestation. Between June 2000 and June 2008 more than 150 000 square kilometers of rain forest were cleared in the Brazilian Amazon. As the rainforests of the world disappear so do thousands of plants that have medicinal and healing powers. According to a recent estimate, over 5,000 different species of medicinal herbs and plants exist at present in rainforests worldwide. These plants have been used by healers, shamans, and other tribal people for thousands of years, but could now vanish if we don't take action to save them.

Yupik Grandmother Rita says that her people have used plant medicines from the land for thousands of years. Their healers know exactly what and how to treat with the plants and know all the side effects. Because they haven't been scientifically approved, the world can't use them. Grandmother Rita "talks" with the plants, asking them to tell her how to use them for healing, and she has discovered that the information she gets is similar to the knowledge given to her by her elders. Indigenous peoples are the guardians of the forest and the medicines, and are appointed by nature, the Grandmothers say. No one should be allowed to come in, take their knowledge, and transform it into commercial patents, with the probable destruction to the forest. Whatever is taken out the forest must be done in the spirit of an equal and respectful exchange, and only after consultation with indigenous peoples, the caretakers of the forest.

Plant Spirits

For most humans, plants don't think or have feelings. However, it has been documented that plants react to music, especially soothing music. In 1967, I was invited by a medium to a spiritualist church in Watts, California, two years after the August 1965 riots in Watts. I was greeted by an all-black congregation with open arms and presented with a plant. At first I didn't understand the significance of the plant until they explained that each member had a plant to pray over.

The church was filled with large, healthy plants. How could these plants grown so large by mere prayer alone, I wondered. Soon, the minister and the medium explained that all life has consciousness and responded to love and positive energy, like humans. It was a spiritual lesson I'd never forget.

Western Shoshone spiritual leaders Corbin Harney said it best, "We have to come back to the Native way of life. The Native way is to pray for everything, to take care of everything. We see what's taking place: the animal life has begun to show us, the tree life is showing us, and the water is even telling us, but we're not paying attention to it.

"People today don't realize that what's out there—all the things growing on the land—needs to have our prayers. These things are here on the Earth with us. We're part of their life too, and together this is how we are to survive over the long term."

In the PBS documentary, *What Plants Talk About*, experimental plant ecologist Dr. J.C. Cahill made some astonishing information about plants and how they eavesdrop on each other, talk to their allies, call on insect mercenaries and nurture their young. We think of plants as none-thinking, none-hearing, none-seeing, yet they can find their own food, communicate with each other and even wage war. If a plant is injured or under attack by insects, animals or even humans, they put out a chemical S.O.S. Like all of Earth's nature, life has evolved for survival of the fittest. Even without eyes, a brain, ears, plants do communicate through chemicals they release—it's just that modern humans have forgotten how complex and evolved they truly are.

It has been documented that plants are capable of "intent" and an emotional response. They respond to the world around them, to bees, to insects, to sunlight and darkness, to wind, to drought and rains. Have you ever noticed that a dandelion, a profuse weed, can grow anywhere? In the wild the dandelion grows to several feet high, yet when it grows in your yard it stays only high enough to escape the lethal blades of your lawn mower. Dandelions are very clever and have adapted well.

One of the first scientists to describe plants as having consciousness was a Viennese biologist named Raoul Francé. He stated that plants were capable of astonishing perception and even communication. He further felt that plants reacted to abuse and appeared thankful for kindness. Scientists in the early twentieth century ignored Francé's findings, but in the 1960s his findings were confirmed by researchers who proved that plants do possess the ability to communicate to humans.

Another scientist to understand the complexity of plants was Luther Burbank (1849-1926), who was well-known for plant cross-pollination and selective breeding. He stated that "the secret of improved plant breeding is love." One of his extraordinary experiments was the development of the spineless cactus, which was used for the feeding of livestock. Burbank said he spoke gently to the cacti, thereby letting them know they would not need their thorns. By creating an environment of love and trust, he was able to eventually breed a new thornless variety. (I wonder if the plant was truly happy with that outcome!).

In 1939, a man named Semyon Kirlian accidently discovered that if an object on a photographic plate was connected to a high-voltage source, an image appeared on the photographic plate. Kirlian photography, although the study of which can be traced back to the late 1700s, was officially invented in 1939 by Semyon Davidovitch Kirlian. The Kirlian photographic process revealed visible "auras" around the objects photographed. These photographs became the subject of great skepticism and controversy over the years.

The process involved a sheet of photographic film placed on top of a metal plate. The object to be photographed was then placed on top of the film. To create the initial exposure, high voltage current was then applied to the metal plate. The electrical coronal discharge between the object and the metal plate was captured on film, producing a glowing aura around the silhouetted object as a result of developing the film.

Kirlian and his wife Valentina didn't make their discovery known until 1958, but it took until 1970 for the phenomenon to become widely known. During this time, Kirlian photography expanded into photographs of human subjects, animals and just about anything else.

Results of scientific experiments published in 1976 involving Kirlian photography of living tissue (human finger tips) showed that most of the variations in corona discharge streamer length, density, curvature and color can be accounted for by the moisture content on the surface of and within the living tissue.

In the early 1970s I had the good fortune of meeting Dr. Thelma Moss, a psychology professor at UCLA's Neuropsychiatric Institute (NPI), later renamed the Semel Institute, through a mutual friend. Dr. Moss and the NPI had a laboratory dedicated to parapsychology research and staffed mostly with volunteers. I had hoped to be one of her volunteers, but unfortunately distance and work prevented me from getting involved. Eventually the lab was shut down by the university. Toward the end of her tenure at UCLA, Dr. Moss became interested in Kirlian photography.

I deeply regret not accepting Dr. Moss's offer to volunteer at the lab and learn more about Kirlian photograph and the human aura from this amazing woman. Dr. Moss also explored a wide range of specific subjects in parapsychology such as hypnosis, ghosts, levitation and alternative medicine.

Places like England, Ireland and Scotland have long been known for their legends and folklore of fairies, elves, devas and elementals; nature's spirits that dwell in the forests. They are the unseen intelligences who inhabit the four elements (Air, Earth, Fire and Water), which they were made from. According to Theosophists Charles Webster Leadbeater and Alice A. Bailey, suggested that devas represent a separate evolution to that of humanity. The concept of devas as nature-spirits derives from the writings of Theosophist Geoffrey Hodson. Theosophists believe there are numerous different types of devas with a population in the millions performing different functions on Earth to help the ecology function better. It is asserted they can be observed by those whose third eyes have been activated.

In addition, it is believed by Theosophists that there are millions of devas living inside the Sun, the indwelling solar deity of which Theosophists call the "Solar Logos"—these devas are called solar angels, or sometimes solar devas or solar spirits. It is believed they visit Earth and can be observed, like other devas, by humans when the third eyes have been activated. Theosophists believe that there are also devas living inside all the other stars besides the sun and they are called stellar angels.

Findhorn Story

Findhorn is a remarkable story of plants. It all started when Dorothy Maclean moved to London in 1953 to study under spiritual leader Sheena after going through a divorced two years earlier. There she joined Peter and Eileen Caddy, managers of the Cluny Hill Hotel in Forres, four miles from Findhorn. The hotel prospered and so they were sent to another hotel to duplicate their success, but they found working conditions impossible and asked to return to Cluny Hill. All three people were fired.

The year was 1962 and they moved to the trailer park near the village of Findhorn. They meditated daily for work, but there was none to be found. Soon they found unemployment benefits didn't provide enough to survive on. That's when Peter decided to garden, although the soil was barren at the time, mostly sand and gravel.

Peter and Eileen Caddy had to build soil using techniques such as cutting seaweed from the rocks and hauling buckets of horse manure and wood ash. Meanwhile, Dorothy discovered that by listening to the plants or plant devas, while tuning into her God self, she could connect to them. To their astonishment, the plants began to grow beyond their wildest expectations. Findhorn became famous for giant vegetables growing under seemingly impossible conditions, like a 42-pound cabbage. Herbs, fruit trees and flowers found in warmer climates grew and thrived.

According to reports, horticulture experts were puzzled how the plants could grow in such harsh, almost impossible terrain. The British Soil Association and other experts visited Findhorn searching for answers. People flocked there to become a part of the spiritual community, and by 1973 Findhorn had grown to a community of over 200 people.

Later that year, Dorothy was guided to return to North America working with David Spangler and the group that began the Lorian Association. She stayed in the Pacific Northwest for many years. Now in her nineties, Dorothy retired from public life and returned to her beloved Findhorn. She is the author of *Seeds of Inspiration: Deva Flower Messages*, *To Honor the Earth: Reflections of Living in Harmony with Nature, Choices of Love, Call of the Trees* and *To Hear the Angels Sing*.

I have always believed that for every illness and disease there is a plant, tree or herb that heals. Ancient people knew the magical and medicinal properties of all plants in their land and when to harvest the plant—full moon or new moon. They spoke to the plant, said prayers to honor its power and then prepared it for the person ailing.

House plants grown in a loving environment, nurtured, spoken to, send out a response to human kindness. Outdoor plants and trees want the same respect. The plant kingdom is very generous when shown great respect and move and bend in the direction of love expressed.

It is believed that there are plants when ingested connect us to other forms of self and consciousness. They are known as hallucinogenic plants. For eons shamans and medicine people have used certain sacred plants to explore other planes of existence. Earth Mother in all her love and integrity grows these plants so that humans can understand the Living Library. There have been those who do not want everyone knowing certain truths, and have told us that these natural plants are bad. One such plant from South America is ayahuasca that gives the user spiritual revelations regarding their purpose on Earth, the true nature of the universe as well as deep insight into how to be the best person they possibly can. This is viewed as a spiritual awakening and a rebirth. In addition, it is often reported that individuals feel they gain access to higher spiritual dimensions and make contact with various spiritual or extra-dimensional beings who can act as guides or healers. Author Don Jose Campos claims that people may experience profound positive life changes subsequent to consuming ayahuasca.

Peyote is another plant used to access dimensional realities. It is a small, spineless cactus with psychoactive alkaloids, particularly mescaline. From earliest recorded time, peyote has been used by indigenous peoples, such as the Huicho of northern Mexico and by various Native American tribes, native to or relocated to the Southern Plains states of present-day Oklahoma and Texas.

There are plants our Western world has never heard of, but used by indigenous people deep within rain forests. Some of these plants could cure all cancers and other diseases if they were harvested in love and in the spirit of higher good. The Living Library of Mother Earth is waiting for the day we awaken to her gifts. When we awaken to the love frequency, the frequency of pure white light, we will transform the entire planet, and the planet will become that vibration.

While visiting Belize on my second trip, my friend Michael and I visited a medicine woman near the Jaguar reserve in the rainforest. She had a store in the front where she sold amber used for incense, beaded jewelry, baskets and other Maya hand-crafted items. We were there to collect an herbal remedy for our friend in Idaho who had been diagnosed with stage four lung cancer. She recited several prayers over the powered substance, put it in a plastic bag, and gave us verbal instructions on how the medicine should be taken.

Our friend tried the herbal remedy, but sadly, he passed away—the cancer had metastasized to other areas of his body. I only wished we had been able to get the medicine long before the cancer had advanced. I believe he might have beaten it.

The plight of the non-Indian world is that it has lost respect for Mother Earth, from whom and where we all come. —Ed McGaa "Eagle Man" Oglala Sioux Ceremonial Leader

CHAPTER SEVEN
Animal Spirits

Indigenous cultures speak of the mystery and communication between human and Mother Nature's creatures. Animals are psychic and can predicted extreme weather and sense earthquakes and other disasters long before they happen. Stories abound of dogs and cats that have the ability to predict earthquakes, predict their owner's death and forewarn humans of a disaster. They have even been known to travel great distances to find their owner.

I've had many pets since childhood—cats, dogs, horses, a rabbit, a turtle, and two birds, an owl and robin I nursed back to health. Each pet had a unique personality and intelligence. There were even times when I felt a telepathic link with them. I know in my heart that animals have souls and when they die they join us on the Other Side. They even reincarnate and join us on great adventures lifetime after lifetime. I've always believed that everything is evolving and growing spiritually, including all life forms visible and invisible.

Buddhists have always regarded animals as sentient beings. Animals possess Buddha nature and have the potential for enlightenment like all consciousness. Buddhists believe in rebirth, and that any human could be reborn as an animal, and any animals could be reborn as a human. They also take the concept a bit further and believe that sentient beings currently residing in the animal realm have been our mothers, brothers, sisters, father, children, and friends in past lives.

Animals were given to us on Mother Earth as companions and teachers, even those we eat. If animals killed for food were taken with love and respect, then the animal spirit would gladly give up its physical body. But presently, we do not honor the animals we eat; instead they are treated as if they were not alive, as if they don't feel pain and have intellect. A great many animals on this planet are abused and with it comes a great karmic lesson. Perhaps if we all held all living creatures in reverence like Buddhist monks, life on this planet would have evolved much faster. Buddhist monks even try to avoid accidently killing insects, and if they do happen to step on a bug, they pray for its soul.

Ed McGaa "Eagle Man" says, "If I take a four legged or catch a finned, I tell it that I am taking it to provide and I thank it. Many finned I put back into the water and let them go." It is this relationship with all living things that we must honor again.

There are stories animals were brought here from other planets where they were evolved sentient beings. They were biogenetically engineered to be our companions and to seed Earth. In ancient Egypt the cat, both small and large, were considered deities because they held great information and monitored their human family. Is it any wonder that lions and cats cover the walls of ancient temples? The ancients believed cats were transmitters to extraterrestrial species.

After years of owning a number of wonderful cats, I've seen how telepathic they can be. Dogs are just as intuitive. Isn't it ironic how our pets know what time we'll arrive home from work? Our cat Comet saved my husband and me late one night. Comet appeared upset, going in and out of his cat door from the living room to the garage. That wasn't like him. My husband finally got up to see what the commotion was all about and made a shocking discovery in our garage—gasoline had leaked from our VW camper bus and was moving toward the gas heater. If Comet hadn't persisted in getting our attention, I can only imagine the disastrous consequences.

Not long ago I found Comet with his fur on end, hissing and staring up at a photograph of my departed sister Kathy in the hallway. I know Kathy was there in spirit. There had been other confirmations of her presence during that time.

According to the ancients animals exist in two realities—our 3-D world and the spirit world, and access both world all day and night. At this time animals are mirroring the pain humans are feeling psychologically, spiritually and physically. That's why our pets have cancers, obesity and diabetes. They are mirroring what we need to learn about ourselves. When we learn that what we do to ourselves, we do to the planet and all life, and then we will be ready to sit in council with beings of higher planes. We will finally comprehend how the God force exists in all things. We will learn that as humans we aren't the only intelligent species or the most evolved.

Elephants grieve for the death of their own, dogs and cats have been known to grieve for their owners and other animals. Perhaps the most enticing quality of elephants is their undeniable similarity to humans: they have close bonds they form with family members, they communicate with each other, they have a long life span, the care and protect their young, they have great intelligence and they have emotions—many of the same emotions as people do. Elephants are capable of sadness, joy, love, jealousy, fury, grief, compassion and distress. Moreover, we see these same attributes in our pets.

When an elephant dies, the herd will take great care in the burial. Cows walk to and fro in search of leaves and twigs to cover the body of the deceased in an act of dignity for the dead. When a herd encounters the skeleton of a dead elephant, they have shown a great fascination for the skeleton as the cows caress the bones. The cows then take the bones and scatter them, hiding them under bushes in the surrounding area. Even years later, elephants have been observed revisiting the place where one of their family members died. They will remain there for days at a time, in mourning.

There are stories of whales and dolphins guiding ships and dolphins saving humans adrift in the ocean. Sadly, a great number of the cetaceans are taken from their families and mothers and put into small tanks for human entertainment. Whales and dolphins are part of a huge social group of sea creatures, in which individuals are dependent upon each other. Remove them from both these aspects of their lives, and the claustrophobic effects upon them can become catastrophic. Depression, physical illness and aberrant behavior have all been revealed in the 2013 documentary *Blackfish*. The documentary focused on Tilikum, an orca held by SeaWorld and the controversy over the captive killer whale, which ended in the death of three people. Taking these giants of the water from their mothers and placing them in small pools to perform tricks for large crowds is inhuman and abusive.

In addition, those orcas taken into captivity from the wild are not the only ones that suffer. The pods that are left behind may depend upon them for many social reasons, and vital bonds necessary for orca survival can be broken as key members are taken from family groups. Orcas and dolphins taken from their pods can never be reintroduced to the wild again. They become outcasts and can never rejoin a pod again. The movie *Free Willy,* was not based on fact!

Animals of the world do not belong in cages for human entertainment. They need to be respected and honored and left to enjoy their freedom. Whenever humans interfere with nature, introduce a new species to nature, whether animals or plant, the consequences are usually disastrous. Nature has its own perfect balance.

Animal Sixth Sense

Witnesses reported that shortly before the 9.3 megathrust earthquake hit Indonesia on December 26, 2004, animals such as elephants and monkeys rushed for higher ground, and cattle, dogs and domestic animals showed anxiety. Surprisingly, few dead animals were recovered after the tsunami hit coastal areas, but 230,000 human lives were lost that day.

Whether animals have a sixth sense or just feel unusual vibrations or changes in air pressure coming from one direction is debatable among researchers. If a herd of animals are seen fleeing before an earthquake, all that is needed is for one or two of them to skittishly sense danger. When you think about it, we shouldn't be surprised by animal sixth sense. Feral animals have excellent senses of smell, sight, hearing and even the ability to sense minute vibrations, because they've evolved those senses in order to survive. Many species perceive and use electromagnetic fields to navigate or find prey that are imperceptible to humans.

A few years ago I watched the award-winning documentary *The Animal Communicator,* about Anna Breytenbach, a South African-based professional animal communicator who received advanced training through the Assisi International Animal Institute in California, USA. Born and raised in Cape Town, South Africa, she holds a degree in Psychology, Economics and Marketing from the University of Cape Town. Anna lives out her passion for wildlife and conservation by volunteering at various rehabilitation and educational centers.

Anna has dedicated her life to what she calls "interspecies communication." In the documentary Anna was asked to help with a black leopard living at the South Africa's Jukani Wildlife Sanctuary. The Olsens, the young couple who owners of the Jukani Wildlife Sanctuary, had taken in a vicious snarling black leopard from Europe called Diablo. They had other wild cats in their care, and never had any problem with them until Diablo came to their sanctuary. After six months in the sanctuary, Diablo never left his night shelter. He hissed and snarled, and even bit Mr. Olsen's hand once, landing him in the hospital for a week. He and his wife didn't want to get rid of Diablo, but they didn't know what to do with him.

Anna was then called in to help without any prior knowledge of the cat. What happened next was nothing short of miraculous. As soon as Anna came near the angry leopard, he instantly calmed down and let her knell beside his cage. As the big cat and Anna stared into each other eyes, she began to sense the leopard was awed by his new surroundings but still stressed by the treatment he received at his prior residence. She sensed the beautiful leopard had been abused and had become wary of humans.

Anna believed the leopard had both physical power and great wisdom and personality that commanded respect—but not in a needy way. After communicating with Diablo, it was established that he didn't understand that he was safe there, and free to roam, relax and be at ease. He told Anna that he didn't like the name, Diablo—that wasn't who he was. It brought forth negativity and darkness.

Diablo then asked Anna about the two young cubs that were at the zoo, something she had not been told about. Both Mr. and Mrs. Olsen were stunned by his information—they had not told Anna that Diablo had been with two small cub leopards at the zoo.

In the following days, the Mr. and Mrs. Olsen changed Diablo's name to "Spirit" and shortly afterward, the great cat began to explore his new surroundings and go outside to his night shelter. One day Mr. Olsen decided to talk to Spirit, and told him he was safe there, that they would make no demands of him. He began telling Spirit how beautiful he was, and each time the big cat would reply in a low growl. This went on nineteen times!

Upon Anna's return to the sanctuary, Mr. Olsen explained the interaction between he and Spirit had one day. Anna explained how appreciative the cat was for the kind words and that surprised him. It made him stop in his tracks. Spirit was replying "thank you" to Mr. Olsen's "beautiful" remarks.

Although a sceptic at first about animal communication, Mr. Olsen was overcome by emotion, filling him with awe he couldn't express in words. That's when he realized that he could also communicate with wild cats. He and his wife have since taken Anna's class on interspecies communication.

Learning to communicate with animals is to practice being present and fully aware with all senses—to be in a state of acceptance, love, trust, gentleness, and calm. It is a form of meditation where we quiet our minds to allow the conversation with other creatures. Sometimes an animal or plant may not want to communicate, and this boundary should be respected. Their language is not our human language. It's a language older than words, transference of thought. Anna in her teachings of interspecies communication says this is our birthright. We all have this ability if learned. It's call intuition.

Many years ago I discovered Chippewa teacher Sun Bear's

book, *The Medicine Wheel: Earth Astrology*. Each astrological sign of the month connected to earth energies, animal totems, minerals and plants. I began incorporating these beautiful lessons into my own psychic readings, and found them to be amazingly accurate.

Sun Bear said the Medicine Wheel came to him in a vision.

I saw a hilltop bare of trees, and there was a soft breeze blowing. The prairie grass was moving gently. Then I saw a circle of rocks that came out like the spokes of a wheel. Inside was another circle of rocks, nearer to the center of the wheel. I knew that here was the sacred circle, the sacred hoop of my people. Inside of the center circle was the buffalo skull, and coming up through ravines, from the four directions, were what looked like animals. As they came closer, I saw that they were people wearing headdresses and animal costumes. They moved to the circle and each group entered it sunwise, making a complete circle before they settled on their place in the wheel.

All the people were singing the song of their season, of their minerals, of their planets, of their totem animals. And they were singing songs for the healing of the Earth Mother. A leader among them was saying, "Let the medicine of the sacred circle prevail. Let many people across the land come to the circle and make prayers for the healing of the Earth Mother. Let the circles of the Medicine Wheel come back.

In this vision were gathered people of all the clans, of all the directions, of all the totems, and in their hearts they carried peace. That was the vision I saw.

We are connected to animal spirits, the elementals, the rocks, the water, and the winged, finned and four-legged creatures. In the realm of multidimensionality and merging, animals are adepts. Animals move through dimensions. Have you ever seen an animal or a bird one minute, and then the next second it vanished?

Animals are very concerned with the quality of life—much more so than humans are. When the quality of life is in question, animals automatically migrate toward a more sustaining reality. They remove themselves into other domains of existence, for they are programmed to survive.

Animals are intelligent and flexible and have many more adventures than humans do. Animals don't need to build shopping malls, graveyards, watch television and movies, and distract themselves with superficial forms of entertainment. Do you think animals ever get bored? Do you think animals ever wonder what to do next? They have many, many adventures that you are not quite capable of understanding, though you will one day.

Insects and frogs, for example, open dimensional avenues with their sounds. Others may travel on sound. Everything dreams, journeying into many realities. You can best relate to the concept of dreaming knowing that, when you sleep, you go into another world that does exist. Everything exists because it is connected, whether memory is open or not. Beetles, earthworms, and frogs know they go from one reality to another. They go into other worlds, yet they are right here in this world.

Insects work with us in a way we cannot conceive at this time. You think they just accidently land or crawl on you, when in actuality they are checking out your electromagnetic frequency. You do not look like yourself to insects. You are a force field, and there are certain parts of you that are very attractive to insects because of pheromones you give off.

There are many forms of life that will come to awareness and existence. You will want to capture these forms of life and put them in a zoo. To them, you are in the zoo, like a prison, locked behind bars. They want to assist you and bring you back to interspecies communication. They are waiting to see if you can relate to particular animals or species. As you demonstrate your acknowledgment of intelligence in all forms of life, you begin to qualify as an ambassador or diplomatic representative of these various species. Life will become very strange indeed.

When a frog makes a croaking sound, it creates an opening to other dimensions for the animal kingdom—for insects in particular, but for many members of the animal kingdom. Frogs and insects keep frequency and have certain abilities. Frogs, when they croak in the stillness of the day or night, create a harmonic and a spinning momentum. Surrounding energies can move into this sound and experience what it is like to be other forms of life quite easily.

All animals are much more in tune with multiple realities than humans are, and they can teach you about these realities. Some people are able to merge with animals and explore the animal kingdom to discover what it is like to be in the Living Library. Many very intelligent forms of life can manifest themselves by merging with the animal and plant kingdoms.

You see, all life plays a major part in holding the balance of Mother Earth when they tone—the sounds they make. They help hold Earth's grid together.

In this way, animals and insects can peek into your reality. Now these many intelligent forms of life want to merge with humans. As we prepare ourselves to merge with other forms of sentient existence, you will be able to bring peace to Mother Earth. You will be able to bring a magnificent new upliftment, a new way of being, a new prayer, and a new reverence. It will seem as if it is coming out of you, and yet you will know that it is more than you. Understand that there is great intelligence in all life forms, and the experience of all life is waiting for you.

Open your emotional selves and employ the vital force of love as key to your own spiritual evolution. Realize that all life is evolving in the Universe, and animals have souls. Those who harm or abuse animals think their actions won't count in the spiritual scheme of things, but they are wrong. Every word, every action, every thought is recorded in the Akashic records and there is retribution.

When you drive, be sure to put up invisible barriers by asking your Spirit Guides to allow you to drive safely and never hit or injure an animal. Whenever I drive long distances I always say a prayer for protection and it works!

Remember—All LIFE SHOULD ALWAYS BE HONORED, CHERISHED AND RESPECTED.

Native North American Prayer

Do not stand at my bier and weep. I am not there, I do not sleep. I am a thousand winds that blow, I am the diamond glints on snow, I am the sun on ripened grain, I am the gentle autumn's rain. When you awaken in the morning's hush, I am the swift, uplifting rush of Quiet birds in circled flight. I am the soft stars that shine at night. Do not stand at my bier and cry; I am not there, I cannot die.

Native American Prayer

I give you this one thought to keep-
I am with you still,
I do not sleep.
I am a thousand winds that blow,
I am the diamond glints on the snow,
I am the sunlight on ripened grain,
I am the gentle autumn rain.
When you awaken
in the morning's hush,
I am the swift, uplifting rush
of quiet birds in circled flight.
I am the soft stars
that shine at night.
Do not think of me as gone-
I am with you still,
in each new dawn.

Brothers and sisters, we must go back to some of the old ways if we are going to truly save our Mother Earth and bring back the natural beauty that every person seriously needs, especially in this day of vanishing species, vanishing rain forests, overpopulation, poisoned waters, acid rain, a thinning ozone layer, drought, rising temperatures, and weapons of complete annihilation. —Ed McGaa "Eagle Man" Oglala Sioux Ceremonial Leader

CHAPTER EIGHT
Mineral Spirits

In Chapter One you read about the remarkable Australian aboriginal leader Alinta aka Lorraine Mafi-Williams and the legends her people have passed on for generations. They believe that Earth's minerals should remain inside her to balance the energy grids around the planet. Alinta said that due to the massive mining worldwide, Earth is out of balance and in dire need of help.

Alinta's information makes sense when we consider how huge amounts of oil, gas and minerals are extracted from Mother Earth on a daily basis. I can only imagine that such mining and fracking is creating a perilous situation for Mother Earth as her life-blood is removed from her.

The human body is made up of Earth's minerals—we're connected as her children. Can a human live without blood?

Certainly not, and neither can Mother Earth—she is a living breathing entity, and she has blood in the form of water, oil and gas, and without it she will wither and die.

Earth contains crystals, gold, silver, uranium, platinum and many other gems and minerals. There are power points worldwide where people seek for its energy and healing vibrations. Sedona, Arizona is widely known as one of the most beautiful places on the planet, but it is also known for being a spiritual power center due to the energy that originates from the vortexes. It is said that these vortexes produce some of the most remarkable energy on Earth. For this reason Sedona has many people that are "on the path," which is to say people who are committed to spiritual growth. You will notice a large New Age culture in Sedona, showcasing a variety of spiritual practices and alternative healing.

These vortexes hold electromagnetic properties which contribute to the harmony between all life forms on the planet. It is believed that many of these vortexes have crystals beneath them which contribute to its magnetic, electrical and electromagnetic properties, forming grid lies around the planet. These vortexes help uphold a healthy balance within the body, mind and spirit.

I began collecting rocks as a child, especially river rocks, because they are ancient beings and carry a certain inexplicable power. I was blessed to know Oglala Sioux ceremonial leader, Ed McGaa "Eagleman", and spiritual leader of the Western Shoshone nation, Corbin Harney from Nevada, who talked of mineral beings, Mother Earth consciousness and returning to Earth Wisdom.

Ed spoke of the Oglala people who believe in the omnipotence of *Wakan Tanka* [Great Spirit] and how they wear or carry a small, spherical *wotai* stone carefully rolled up in a wad of sage and deposited neatly in a miniature buckskin pouch no more than an inch in diameter. It is not necessary to carry these stones on one's person every day, only when embarking on an important mission like invoking the supernaturals, one carries the stone with him.

In *Rainbow Tribe,* Ed wrote about two special stones that came into his life. The first stone he wore in a buckskin pouch when he flew 110 combat missions and he was never harmed. According to Bill Eagle Feather, Ed's stone hit the Sun Dance tree when an airplane flew over it. Later, the same stone came into the *Yuwipi* Ceremony that Fools Crow held for Ed before he went to

Vietnam.

The second stone, he still carries on him, which came to him after he pierced in the annual Sioux Sun Dance. Chief Eagle Feather predicted that his first combat *wotai* would leave him after he found his second one in a Black Hills stream.

Ed believes a stone can convey a special meaning to each person when it comes to you in a special way. It may bear special symbols that speak out and assure you that a minute portion of Mother Earth (the stone) was created just for you, millions upon millions of years ago. He also suggests that anyone can find their personal *wotai* stone near the bed of a lake or stream.

Back in the 1990s I found my personal *wotai* stone, a pale-yellow quartz, while walking along the shore of Yellowstone Lake in Yellowstone National Park in Montana. The water was lapping on shore and suddenly I looked down to see a small golden quartz rock shaped like a foot with tiny red veins running through it. As I held the stone, I said a prayer and asked the stone's permission to remove it, and the stone silently gave its permission. I felt the stone was my spirit protector. Now I carry my golden *wotai* stone to keep me safe whenever I travel. With such a simple stone, people can beseech the six powers of Black Elk's message or whatever Higher power concept they may have.

Ed McGaa "Eagle Man" and author in Ketchum, Idaho

The late Chippewa medicine man Sun Bear and his medicine helper, Wabun, authored *The Medicine Wheel: Earth Astrology*, which connects each sign of the zodiac or Medicine Wheel to an animal, plant and mineral.

Sun Bear went on to say that his book, *The Medicine Wheel,* was the result of a vision where for the sake of Earth Mother and all our evolution as human beings, we must return to a better and truer understanding of the Earth and all of our relations on her. "I saw that we would have to put aside the petty fears that divided us and learn to live as true brothers and sisters in a loving way. I saw that we would have to find others who shared our heart's direction, whatever their racial background, and join with them into groups that always remembered that our purpose was to be instruments of the Great Spirit's will and helpers to our Earth Mother. I saw that such groups could affect the cleansing of the Earth that is now occurring."

In writing the book Sun Bear felt that his vision of the Medicine Wheel would help others open their hearts to all of their relations on our common Earth Mother—animal, plant, and mineral kingdom. In honoring Sun Bear and his amazing book, I've included a brief description of minerals and how these minerals and stones relates to each of us on Sun Bear's Medicine Wheel of Life.

Quartz

The quartz rock is the mineral for those born during the Earth Renewal Moon (Snow Goose) December 22 – January 19 (Capricorn). Quartz is composed of silicon dioxide. It comes in almost any color but the most common is clear or white. Quartz is a stone believed to hold power. It is used today in radio, radar, television, ultrasonics and other fields as a transmitting force. Kings and nobles carried scepters with quartz crystal on top. Atlantis, according to the late seer Edgar Cayce, had a giant crystal that generated huge energy. Eventually that energy proved to be the destruction of Atlantis. Crystal balls used by psychics to see the future were made of clear quartz. Tribes in Australia used quartz in their rain-making ceremonies and Native American tribes used quartz for healing. Those born during this time can use quartz to see more clearly and they must learn not to become too hardened in their beliefs or they can crack like quartz.

Have you ever experienced piezoelectricity? By striking two

crystals together (be sure to wear protective glasses) you'll see flashes of light. Natural occurring piezoelectricity might explain the phenomenon known as earthquake lights that appear in the sky near areas of tectonic stress, seismic activity, or volcanic eruptions. It is theorized that these lights are created by tectonic movement of rocks containing quartz deep within Earth.

Silver
Silver is the mineral for those born under the Rest and Cleansing Moon (Otter) January 20 – February 18 (Aquarius). Silver is one of the most sought-after minerals and has always been considered one of Earth's most precious metals. The color silver for Otter people is considered to have many magical properties. It is believed a silver cord holds the soul to the body. Grandmother Moon is associated with the metal silver because she appears to have a silvery light when we gaze at her. Because of this association, silver is considered to enhance the powers of the moon, the powers of intuition and emotional energy. Otter people are visionaries—always looking to the future.

Turquoise

The blue-green mineral turquoise is connected to those born during the big Winds Moon (Cougar) February 19 – March 20 (Pisces). The turquoise stone is one of the oldest stones used for adornment and protection. The ancient Egyptians mined turquoise at least six thousand years before the beginning of the Christian era and on this continent at least one thousand years. Native people refer to turquoise as the "skystone" and believed its power could protect them from injury or danger, and so they used it in shields. Navajos used to throw turquoise in the river with prayers to bring about rain for their crops. Apaches believed that turquoise could be found at the end of the rainbow. Other tribes would fasten a turquoise bed to a bow or arrow, believing the arrow would find its target. Like their stone, Cougar people can possess many powers outside the ordinary. They have a lot of natural medicine that can make them adept at many of the mysteries of life and the universe.

Fire Opal

The fire opal is connected to those born during the Budding Trees

Moon (Red Hawk) March 21 – April 19 (Aries). Opal is found in sedimentary rock and in volcanic rock. It is also found near hot springs deposits and it comes in all tints with a glassy to waxy luster. Opals are very fragile, like those born at this time. Opal containing flashes of light are known as fire opals and are the rarest and most beautiful variety. Ancient people believed an opal offered hope and could make the wearer invisible at times. With the opal's fire, it was believed the stone was connected to the powers of the sun, the moon and fire. Like the opal, Red Hawk people are sensitive and their spirits can be stained by the wrong ideas or if they are associated with the wrong people. They can fracture easily in the wrong situations. But in the right situation they burn with a great energy and passion. Red Hawk people, like their mineral, are often the symbol of hope for any new idea. They can set ideas in motion.

Chrysocolla

Chrysocolla is the mineral associated with those born during the Frogs Return Moon (Beaver) April 20 – May 20 (Taurus). This stone is similar to turquoise. It is often found as a by-product of the copper mining process like turquoise. It ranges from true green to greenish blue to a true blue color. It has been used for adornment since early times, although it was not valued like turquoise. The blue color is said to balance the wearer of the stone to the elements of Earth and sky within. It is considered a stone that can purify the heart, mind and spirit. From the stone, Beaver people can learn to connect themselves to the power of Earth Mother and the sky. Sometimes Beaver people are too rooted to the Earth, and forget to look skyward to see what lessons there are for them in this plane of existence. The blue shade of the chrysocolla can be a great reminder for these people to balance themselves in both the material and spiritual world.

Moss Agate

Moss agate is the mineral associated with those born during the Cornplanting Moon (Deer) May 21 – June 20 (Gemini). The bands of color throughout the stone make it appear as if it contains preserved moss. The moss agate is a healing stone and considered beneficial for the eyes. But it has also been used to heal other parts of the body in a pendulum style. There are people who carry moss agate with them to experience its healing properties. Due to its color it is believed to be linked to the mineral and plant kingdom, enabling its owner to have a better understanding of both kingdoms. Ancient peoples believed that moss agate quenched their thirst if a small pebble was placed in their mouth. It was also believed that the moss agate had the power to bring about rain for the plants when needed. Like the moss agate, Deer people have healing abilities.

Carnelian Agate

Carnelian agate is associated with the Strong Sun Moon (Flicker) June 21 – July 22 (Cancer). Carnelian is a clear chalcedony, which can range in color from pink to red to yellow. The yellow variety is usually referred to as *sard*. The opaque form of these stones is jasper. In ancient times the stone was used for jewelry and other ornaments. Its color was associated with blood and considered to be an emergency stone for anyone injured. It was said to stop the flow of blood from wounds. The stone is also linked to the heart. For those born under the Strong Sun Moon, their hearts are home oriented, and they function best at home. They too, can be very intuitive.

Garnet

Garnet and iron are the stones associated with the Ripe Berries Moon (Sturgeon) July 23 – August 22 (Leo). The gemstone, the garnet, is a silicate crystal, which is fairly hard. Garnet runs from red to brown, green, yellow, black and white. Red is the color most associated with garnet, and red is the color of Sturgeon people—associated with the moon. It is also associated with the heart and the blood. Long ago people ground up the garnet into a poultice as a stimulant for the heart. There was a belief that a garnet bullet could always penetrate the heart of an enemy. Garnet was also believed to have power to balance sexual energies.

Iron is also associated with Sturgeon people. It is one of the hardest minerals. Iron is found in the human body and is also the central ion in the hemoglobin molecule which is needed for survival. Celtics believed that the Iron Age caused fairies and other magical little folks to turn their backs on humans.

Amethyst
Amethyst is the stone associated with the Harvest Moon (Brown Bear) August 23 – September 22 (Virgo). Amethyst is a form of quartz usually lilac, purple or violet in color and is transparent. It is found worldwide and can be traced back to the ancient Egyptian pharaohs and their jewelry and the ancient Maya and Aztec empires. Even Cleopatra wore a signet ring of amethyst with an engraving of Mithas, the ancient Persian deity.

The stone is considered to be symbolic of good judgment, justice and courage. The stone was believed to protect its wearer from black witchcraft, as well as lightning and hailstorms. Today many people wear an amethyst crystal to achieve spiritual enlightenment or meditate on.

Jasper
Jasper is associated with the Ducks Fly Moon (Raven) September 23 – October 23 (Libra). Jasper comes in many colors—brown, reddish brown, black, blue, yellow, green and combinations known as picture jasper. Moon people are most associated with the bloodstone jasper which was used by the ancients in Egypt, Babylon, and China. It was believed that jasper has the power to give forth the heat of the sun and if placed it water, caused water to boil.

Ancient people believed the stone held magical powers and had the power to stop bleeding, to make its owner invisible, to ensure a safe and long life, and to draw poison from a snakebite, and to restore lost eyesight and to bring rain if placed in water. It was used to ward off bad spirits and to allow the wearer to cast spells on others. Jasper is believed to attract Earth energy.

Copper
Copper and malachite are associated with those born during the Freeze Up Moon (Snake) October 24 – November 21 (Scorpio). Copper is found worldwide and from the earliest times was used for implements and ornamentation. Copper is attributed to a wide variety of special powers like purification of the spirit and blood. For ages people have used copper bracelets or anklets to alleviate stiff joints, painful arthritis and rheumatism.

Today copper conducts electricity better than most other minerals, and it is used in wiring for this energy. It also is used in on the bottom of pans to spread heat evenly for cooking. In older times copper was used with crystal to focus energies for seeing into the future.

Malachite is also the gemstone of Snake people and is found in copper mines. It is usually bright green color. It is linked to spiritual powers and used in vases, ornaments and statues. It is considered a stone that increases your receptivity to all forms of energy and increases psychic powers.

Obsidian

Obsidian is linked to those born during the Long Snows Moon, (Elk) November 22 – December 21 (Sagittarius). Obsidian is the mineral linked to Elk people, and is volcanic glass. Obsidian can be found throughout the world in Italy, New Zealand, Mexico, Iceland, Scotland, Peru, Canada, Kenya, Japan, Argentina, Chile and most of the Western United States near lava flows. Black obsidian is hard and razor-sharp along its edges, so it was perfect for making arrowheads, spearheads and scrapers for Native people. The Maya formed obsidian into mirrors and beautiful jewelry, including cylinder earplugs so thin they are transparent as glass. The ancient Egyptians also carved obsidian into statutes and decorative pieces.

Because obsidian comes from deep within Mother Earth, it is thought to have the power to ground people to the Earth energy, teaching them how to respect and use this energy within. Obsidian is also believed to give the wearer telepathic powers to read a person's thoughts. Because of this ability, obsidian has often been used as a scrying stone, one that allows people to see into the future. Obsidian was also believed to protect the wearer against evil spirits.

This is just a small sampling of Sun Bear's vision and wisdom in *The Medicine Wheel: Earth Astrology*, and how certain animals, plants and minerals relate to each of us.

Sun Bear and Wabun said they wanted each of us to find our place on the Medicine Wheel, to identify with powers that may have been lost to the modern world. They wanted us to find the kinship with the universe so that all can understand why Native people understood and practiced this knowledge. They reminded us that when we completely blend with all things, then we are truly part of the whole. If humanity is to evolve, then we must all come closer to understanding our environment. Due to man's alienation from natural things, he has created his own illnesses. It was there vision that people would return to the natural balance of life again, and honor everything. They believed, *"If we open our hearts, the light of the love and unity that created the universe can shine in and illuminate the flat and arid landscape in which we sometimes choose to live. If we start traveling the magic circle, our hearts will naturally begin to open wider as we learn to experience this life we have been given in all of its beautiful aspects."*

So-called "miracles" occur every time a genuine spirit calling ceremony takes place. I think these "miracles" could be termed communications because they are phenomena wherein holy persons or spiritual leaders have the ability to communicate into the spirit world. —Ed McGaa "Eagle Man" Oglala Sioux Ceremonial Leader

CHAPTER NINE
Spirit

I'm sure most of you watched the 2004 hit movie, *What the Bleep Do We Know* that made us question our reality and our relationship in it. It awakened our limited beliefs and opened up a new world of quantum physics. We can no longer look at the world as real and consistent—now we look at the world with both new and ancient eyes. Now we are discovering what our ancestors, shamans and indigenous people have known for thousands of years—an unseen world exists beside our physical world.

There is a view that we live in a three-dimensional, infinite volume universe that is one of an infinite number of infinite volume of universes that live in an infinite volume four-dimensional hyperspace. There is speculation that 3D universes are all in random motion, relative to one another, and in motion relative to the 4D hypervolume. It gets even more complicated: the study of these universes are given in terms of m-brane theory, non-compactified N-dimensional Kaluza-Klein spaces, and Quaternionic or Clifford spaces.

Some of these hyperdimensional overlappings of one or more 3D universes, may last some finite time. These overlappings could allow, on occasion, for materials and entities from the inter-involved 3D universes to "feed-through" into other 3D universes. For a layperson, like myself, this means there are "dimension doors." The majority of these are ephemeral, lasting small fractions of a second, but there also exist more permanent overlappings, which reside in one particular spot year after year. Such locations that I mentioned earlier in the book can be found globally, known as "stargates."

It is conceivable that a human being might be able to pass into these "stargates" and end up in another universe or dimension. It's also conceivable that if these doorways last for a second and close again, the trip might be a one-way affair. There are a great number of weird and unexplainable stories of people, armies, planes, and ships that have simply vanished without a clue to their whereabouts. There are also stories of people who are walking down a road in the present reality and suddenly they are trust into another time.

If such stories are true and humans have slipped into dimensional doorways, could these doorways also allow extraterrestrials and ghosts into our physical world? Are we just a vibrational rate away from other realities and dimensional past and future portals? I have no doubt that such dimensional doorways exist and the ancients were well-versed in these stargates.

Scientists discovered that if you want a time warp simply walk up some stairs. It turns out that time isn't consistent; it actually runs faster in higher places. In a recent experiment, scientists placed two atomic clocks on two tables, then raised one of the tables by 33 centimeters and found out that the higher clock was running faster than the lower one at a rate of a 90-billionth of a second in 79 years. This is called time dilation, and it happens because (as Einstein's theory of relativity predicted) gravity warps time as well as space.

Could this theory account for shamanic visions on mountains?

Do you remember Mark Everett, the band leader for the popular rock group, The Eels? Mark's father, Hugh Everett III, (1930-1982), was an American physicist who first proposed the many-world or parallel worlds theory of quantum physics, which he termed his "relative state" formulation, later renamed *many-worlds*. Everett's many-worlds interpretation asserts that all alternative histories and futures are real, each one existing with our own world. The many-world theory views reality as a many-branched tree, wherein every possible quantum outcome is realized.

Then it might be said that our thoughts create worlds.

Although Everett was ridiculed in his day, he may have been vindicated by the double-slit experiment also known as *Young's Experiment*. During the late 1980s, scientists discovered that using the double slit experiment where electrons and photons are fired through two slit openings on a screen produced some very weird results. Instead of the photons making two patterns on the screen as the scientists thought, they discovered on the other side of the screen that three smudge patterns appeared. They were left scratching their heads about the wave-like interference.

Shamans and holy people have used dreams to enter other realities as well as for spiritual and practical guidance. The ancestors believed the Great Mystery offered the gift of dreamtime to all creatures where we become One. Buddhist priests have long suggested *it is not the dream that commands the dreamer, but the dreamer who commands the dream.*

When you dream at night, your consciousness enters another reality, similar to death. Most often the shaman used the dreamtime to heal and shift the energy of the ill person and to gain knowledge from the spirit world. The dream world can help us navigate through our daily world of stress and it connects us to deeper parts of ourselves, the ancient ancestors, and the past, the present and the future, because the dreaming mind is not limited to physical restraints. The dreaming mind is free to explore other realms and other realities, and isn't tied to time and space like our waking world.

The Tibetans believe in the *bardo* states of existence between lifetimes. Some Buddhist schools teach of six *bardos* or intermediate states. According to Chogyal Namkhai Norbu these states include: the walking state, dream state, meditative state, dying process, the arising of visions as a consequence of one's karmic experiences, and finally the search for rebirth or reincarnation to confront karmic seeds.

From the late 1960s into the early 1980s, Jane Roberts communicated with an energy personality named Seth. For those of you who have never read Jane Robert's book, I can tell you they delve into deep spiritual matters on the natural of reality—long before we used the term "quantum physics."

The channeled entity Seth had a great deal to say about dreams. He explained, "The nature of the thoughts and feeling you originate and those that you habitually or characteristically receive set a pattern, so you will choose from those probable futures, those events that will physically become your experience.

"Because there are bleed-throughs and interconnections, it is possible for you to tune into a 'future event.' Say of an unfortunate nature, an event for which you are headed if you continue on your present course. A dream about it, for instance, may so frighten you that you avoid the event and do not experience it. If so, such a dream is a message from a probable self who did experience the event.

"So can a child then in a dream receive such communication from a probable future self, of such a nature that its life is completely changed? The entire identity is being now. All divisions are merely illusions, so one probable self can hold out a helping hand to another, and through these inner communications the various probable selves in your terms begin to understand the nature of their identity.

"Now this leads to other adventures in which whole civilizations may be involved, for as individuals have their probable destinies, so do civilizations, nations, and inhabited planetary systems. Your historical earth, as you know it, has developed in many different ways, and there is deeply unconscious connection that unites all such manifestations. In some probable realities, Christianity as you know it did not flourish. Suffice it to say, you are surrounded by other influences and events. Certain of these you perceive in your three-dimensional reality. You accept them as real without realizing that they are only portions of other events."

As physicists explore quantum physics, I have no doubt they will discover our three-dimensional world is malleable, and there is an infinite number of unseen worlds that coexist with our own—and those worlds, like our own physical world, were created by pure thought.

Ancient Spirits

Ed McGaa teaches that when holy people conduct ceremonies miracles happen frequently. He believes that indigenous leaders who can reach into the spirit world and receive prediction, knowledge or healing, have one common trait: they are extremely truthful. I have seen Ed conduct ceremony in a sweat lodge, and how he can summon in the spirits. Native Americans continue their ancient ceremonies of communicating with the spirit world, their ancestors.

In Australia, an Aboriginal person's soul or spirit is believed to continue on after our physical form has passed through death. After the death of an Aboriginal person their spirit returns to the Dreamtime from where it will return through birth as a human, an animal, a plant or a rock. The shape is not important because each form shares the same soul or spirit from the Dreamtime.

Indigenous cultures worldwide have honored the spirit world in the form of deities, various unseen beings, angels, ghosts, and the souls of their departed relatives, knowing another realm exists beside our physical world.

The Day of the Dead is a holiday observed throughout Mexico. The holiday focuses on gatherings of family and friends to pray for and remember friends and family members who have died. The Day of the Dead celebration dates back to ancient traditions among pre-Columbian cultures. Rituals celebrating the death of ancestors had been observed by these civilizations perhaps for as long as 2,500–3,000 years. The festival that developed into the modern Day of the Dead fell in the ninth month of the Aztec calendar, about the beginning of August, and was celebrated for an entire month. The festivities were dedicated to the goddess known as the "Lady of the Dead." Each year on October 31, All Hallows Eve, the children make a children's altar to invite the *angelitos* (spirits of dead children) to come back for a visit.

Throughout my life I've experienced spirit communication from my

Spirit Guides and from family members who have passed on. I've always know that the spirit world is real, perhaps more real than our own physical world. How can we ever doubt that the spirit world exists in Mother Earth, the trees, the plants, the birds, the sea creatures, the animals, the rocks, the mountains, the stars, the moon, the sun? Everything radiates the God consciousness.

Spiritual Song of the Australian Aborigine

I am a child of the Dreamtime People
Part of this Land, like the gnarled gumtree
I am the river, softly singing
Chanting our songs on my way to the sea
My spirit is the dust-devils
Mirages, that dance on the plain
I'm the snow, the wind and the falling rain
I'm part of the rocks and the red desert earth
Red as the blood that flows in my veins
I am eagle, crow and snake that glides
Thorough the rain-forest that clings to the mountainside
I awakened here when the earth was new
There was emu, wombat, kangaroo
No other man of a different hue
I am this land
And this land is me
I am Australia.

We have traded the welfare of future generations for immediate profit. Because of spiritual blindness, people look to the bottom line, rather than looking at life. —Grandmother Agnes Baker Pilgrim (Oregon)

CHAPTER TEN
A Dying Planet

In 1971 singer/songwriter Marvin Gaye released *The Ecology* album, which included the haunting song, *Mercy, Mercy Me*. Marvin was a visionary, who realized the disastrous road we were on.

Mercy, mercy me
Ah things ain't what they used to be, no no
Where did all the blue skies go?
Poison is the wind that blows from the north and south and east
Woo mercy, mercy me, mercy
Ah things ain't what they used to be, no no
Oil wasted on the ocean and upon our seas, fish full of mercury
Ah oh mercy, mercy me
Ah things ain't what they used to be, no no

> Radiation under ground and in the sky
> Animals and birds who live nearby are dying
> Oh mercy, mercy me
> Ah things ain't what they used to be
> What about this overcrowded land
> How much more abuse from man can she stand?
> Oh, na na...
> My sweet Lord... No
> My Lord... My sweet Lord

Although Marvin's plea for us to awaken in 1971 was not heeded, I believe there's still time to make changes and start the healing process for future generations. If we give up the fight, all is lost.

Have you ever watched Michael Jackson's 1997 *Earth Song* video? It gives me chills. Michael was addressing us, humanity and society in general. Concerning the fact of what we have done to the Earth, all the forests are being destroyed at an unprecedented rate and the bond we once had with the animals is gone. Because of the ecological unbalance and environmental problems, Earth is dying. The main message by Michael Jackson is for "people to hear the voice of the planet" and encourage people to do something about it. Perhaps the video also represented the coming shift when Earth will be cleansed and renewed—animals will flourish, water and air will be pure again, the trees will reforest the planet and humans will live in peace.

In a paper published in *Science Magazine,* January 2015, Johan Rockström argued that we've already messed up with regards to climate change, extinction of species, addition of phosphorus and nitrogen to the world's ecosystems and deforestation. We are well within the boundaries of ocean acidification and the pollution of freshwater globally. "The planet has been our best friend by buffering our actions and showing its resilience,"Rockström said. "But for the first time ever, we might shift the planet from friend to foe."

Since 2007 the concentration of greenhouse gases in the atmosphere has risen to around 400 parts per million (the 'safe' boundary being 350 parts per million), risking high global temperatures and rising sea levels, droughts and floods and other catastrophic climate problems, currently taking place. But Rockström doesn't see it as all doom and gloom. He is confident that we can step back within some of the boundaries, by slashing carbon emissions and boosting agricultural yields in Africa to soothe deforestation and biodiversity loss.

But there are those who feel that humans aren't doing enough to save the planet. Grandmother Bernadette Rebienot of Gabon, Africa, one of the Thirteen Ingenious Grandmother, said at the International Council held in Phoenicia, New York in October, 2004, "Our planet is sick from the never-ending ravages of people, pollution, deforestation, abusive power, jealousy, and hatred. As the Earth increasingly suffers, we have become more and more disoriented and have lost our way."

Speaking of the events taking place on our planet now with nature, with the toxins in our sky, water, our food and ground, Grandmother Flordemayo said, "The pollutions in a mother is transferred into the womb. The first breast milk an infant receives is tainted with the chemicals the mother has ingested through the years from food, detergents, creams, deodorants, shampoos, cosmetics, hair dyes, including the other pollutions now found in our environment."

Is it any wonder children and adults sometime in their lifetime will have cancer from the poisons in our environment? The travesty of this is humans have a choice to stop the destructive path we are presently on. We can stop the harmful substances manufacturers load into our food, the GMOs, the fluoride in our water, and hormones in our meat and dairy products by refusing to buy any of these products. The future, just like the past, is ours to change.

Grandmother Shinobu Iura of the Amazon Rain Forest of Brazil had a remarkable three-month-long encounter with star beings, who told her they were from another planet, one of an incalculable distance away from Earth. The beings left a message to the people of Earth, an alert, to tell us not to lose ourselves in our material and technological ways, not to forget our spiritual consciousness, not to forget God the great spirit-creator of all things. "They told us to stop disrespecting His creation and to stop the destruction of our planet, which is resulting in the sickness of the Earth and her inhabitants. They told us that this destruction would continue, and that only a change to spiritual consciousness would give hope for our salvation. They warned us that it is necessary to be attentive to products created by technology that can pollute and destroy our terrestrial atmosphere. They said it was necessary to enter into a state of alert. This was twenty-eight years ago [1978], when these questions were not yet so grave."

Grandmother Clara was also told by the beings that she was destined, along with many other conscious people worried about the same issues, to take this message to all the inhabitants of Earth before the grand catastrophe that would bring much destruction and disgrace to all humanity, something already prophesied by peoples with sacred knowledge.

The Grandmothers say the Ancient Ones have told us that it is our job as Earthkeepers to care for Mother Earth and the animals. They believe that the Creator or Great Spirit resides in Mother Earth, the animals, the rocks, the trees, the water, the stars, the sun and the moon. By observing and respecting nature, we learn how to live in balance on our precious planet.

If you don't think our planet is dying, think again! A great debate rages on between scientists whether or not Earth is warming, but it is agreed something profound is happening, whether human caused or natural. Both the National Oceanic and Atmospheric Administration and NASA calculated that in 2014 the world had its hottest year in 135 years of record-keeping. Not only do we have sea stars (starfish) melting and dying *en masse* along the Western Coast of the United States from Alaska to Southern California, but other sea and Earth creatures are disappearing at an alarming rate. Thousands of sea lions are starving to death off the coast of California, deep ocean oarfish, rarely seen, have appeared off the coast of California recently, and sardines have suddenly vanished off the West Coast of California. More than 100,000 young Cassin's auklet seabirds have been found dead since October 2014, from Long Beach, California, to Scott Islands off the northern tip of Vancouver Island, B. C., Canada, where 80% of the Cassins breed some 3.5 million birds. Yet no viruses, bacteria, toxins or other causes of death have been found. The speculation is starvation, but why?

January 22, 2015, dinoflagellates *Noctiluca scintillans* or glowing blue algae, appeared along the seashore of Hong Kong.

This form of algae thrives on nitrogen and phosphorous rich water caused by farm runoffs containing fertilizer and pesticide chemicals. This single-cell life form eats plankton and it itself is eaten by other ocean life forms. But when it glows at night it's a warning that the water is toxic to other life forms. The algae can also glow red, known as "red tide." Scientists say this is a warning to Hong Kong that a dead zone could be coming. Few animals can survive dead zones of oxygen-poor water. And once a dead zone sets in, it's hard for the ocean to recover.

African elephants are poached for their ivory and sold in Asian markets. Once 1.3 million elephants roamed throughout Africa, and now there are only 500,000 remaining on game reserves. Even rhinos are killed for their horns, and gorillas for their hands because certain countries believe these animals will bring them magical and curative powers.

Superstitious beliefs still dominate much of the world today.

Animal Abuse

Animals all around the world continue to be treated without dignity, as if they were unintelligent, unable to reason, to feel pain, and exhibit emotion. Each day there are horrible stories of cattle and dairy cows, horses, dogs, and cats that have been abused or killed from abuse. Even small animals are used in laboratories and experimented on for food products, medicines and cosmetics. Feral animals are hunted for the fun of it, not as a food source. Whales and dolphins are captured in fishing nets or die by large ships in the shipping lanes worldwide. In Japan dolphin pods are herded into Taiji cove and slaughtered during the dolphin hunting season from September to March. Fishermen say the cull is a traditional part of their livelihood in an area that has fished dolphins and whales for thousands of years.

Activists like Yoko Ono, John Lennon's widow, added her voice to the Japanese to stop this dolphin bloodbath. In the Academy award-winning documentary, *The Cove,* activist Ric O'Barry tried to stop the killing, and had his life threatened. As of 2010 the Japanese refused to screen this documentary due to the controversy over the film and the film's subject.

I've always felt that animals should be treated as we want to be treated—with love, dignity and respect. After all, animals have lived on this planet as long or perhaps even longer than humans.

Animals are intelligent and have souls. Every animals and every living thing, including insects, hold the vibration and balance on our planet. The whales and dolphins sing their song and hold the vibration of the oceans, the birds, insects and frogs all tone to Earth Mother and they hold the balance. Without insects on our planet we would not exist. Every living thing has an electromagnetic frequency and with that frequency life depends on each other—a spiritual and necessary symbiotic relationship.

Ancient peoples have considered Mother Earth a living breathing entity, but modern humans have forgotten that our planet allows us the gift of life. We have arrived at the twenty-first century destroying our natural resources at a phenomenal rate without any thought of the consequences, except those few who are trying desperately to stop the destruction of Mother Earth.

Harming Earth Mother

Sir Isaac Newton (1642-1726), English physicist and mathematician, believed that *for every action, there is an equal and opposite reaction*—in other words, Newton understood the universal law of Karma. Karma is what Asian religions believe is the result of an action, good or bad, that will influence a person's future with either happiness or suffering. However, humans have a bad habit of ignoring the ramifications of their actions.

For example, it was April of 2010 deep water oil drilling was taking place in the Gulf of Mexico off the coast of Louisiana when BP's Deepwater Horizon oil rig exploded. It was the largest accidental marine oil spill in the history of the petroleum industry. Following the explosion and sinking of the Deepwater Horizon oil rig, which claimed 11 lives, the sea-floor oil gusher flowed through September 19, 2010. It is estimated that 4.9 million barrels (210 million US gallons) was released into the Gulf of Mexico.

The oil spill was disastrous enough killing hundreds of birds and marine life, but BP began spraying Corexit oil dispersant, a toxic chemical used to dissolve oil spills on the ocean surface. The U.S. government allowed the company to apply chemical "dispersants" to the blossoming oil slick to prevent toxic gunk from reaching the fragile bays, beaches, and mangroves of the coast, where so much marine life originates. But a number of recent studies show that BP and the feds made a huge mistake that has harmed everything from microscopic organisms to bottlenose dolphins.

The problem with the Corexit dispersants was it emulsified into tiny beads, causing them to sink toward the ocean floor. Wave action and wind turbulence degraded the oil further, and evaporation concentrated the toxins in the oil-Corexit mixture, including dangerous compounds called polycyclic aromatic hydrocarbons (PAHs), known to cause cancer and developmental disorders.

When BP began spraying the Gulf, it proved to be toxic to marine life, but when combined with crude oil, the mixture became several times more toxic than oil or dispersant alone. Beaches, wetlands and estuaries became coated in thick oil. The fishing industry came to a halt as people lost their businesses. Those who lived close to the ocean or worked at sea became ill from the toxic oil spill and dispersants. As of 2013 tar balls could still be found on the Mississippi coast, and a 40,000 pound tar mat was discovered near East Grand Terre, Louisiana which prompted closed waters to commercial fishing.

Much of what happened to the Gulf from this disaster has never been fully disclosed to the public and its far-reaching environmental consequences to the Gulf of Mexico. It may take hundreds, maybe thousands of years, before the Gulf is restored to its prior state before the spill. There are reports that the oil still flows into the Gulf of Mexico and was never fully contained.

Everywhere around the world huge amounts of oil and gas are being removed from Mother Earth—her life blood. If we don't find alternative solutions to our energy sources, that won't harm our planet, I fear we'll find, like the Australian Aboriginals believe, the Earth's grid will wobble completely out of balance and the poles will shift. It appears this may be happening to our planet as earthquakes increase in places that aren't known to experience earthquakes; strange booms continue to be heard worldwide along with shaking not related to earthquakes, according to the USGS (US geological survey) earthquake website. Mother Earth is warning us that we can't continue to disrespect her without disastrous consequences.

The great 9.0 magnitude earthquake of Japan happened on Friday, March 11, 2011 at 2:46 pm off the Pacific coast of Tōhoku. It is what scientists call an undersea megathrust earthquake. This earthquake occurred where the Pacific Plate subducted under the plate beneath northern Honshu. The break caused the sea floor to rise by several meters. The earthquake triggered powerful tsunami waves that reached heights of up to 133 feet in Miyako. The earthquake was so powerful it moved Honshu, the main island of Japan, 2.4metres (8' feet) and shifted the Earth on its axis by estimates of between 4 inches and 10 inches. It also generated sound waves detected by the low-orbiting GOCE satellite.

The tsunami destroyed over a million buildings and killed as many as 16,000 (some estimates claim over 19,000 people died that day). The tsunami also caused history's worst nuclear accident, level 7 meltdowns at three reactors at the Fukushima Daiichi Nuclear Power Plant complex, and subsequently warranted the evacuation of hundreds of thousands of residents in a 12-mile radius of the plant. Many electrical generators were taken down, and at least three nuclear reactors suffered explosions due to hydrogen gas that had built up within their outer containment buildings after cooling system failure resulting from the loss of electrical power.

In 2013, Yushi Yoneyama, an official with the Minister of Economy, Trade and Industry, which regulates Tokyo Electric power Co. (TEMPCO), was asked about the radioactive water going into the ocean from Fukushima Plant and he replied, "We think that the volume of water is about 300 tons a day." It is estimated the cleanup from Fukushima will take more than 40 years at a cost of US $11 billion.

We still don't know the total damage the radiation leak had on the ecosystem, but since the 2011 disaster, there have been mysterious die-offs in the Pacific and species like sardines vanishing, deep water oarfish never seen in shallow water, and the inexplicable death of thousands of sea stars along the West Coast from Alaska to California. These sightings may or may not have anything to do with the radiation released into the air and ocean from the Fukushima nuclear plant, but I find it highly suspicious.

Birds are the ideal sentinels for studying potential impacts of radiation to humans because they share many basic biological processes and are easy to observe. For more than a decade scientists have analyzed avian species in another irradiated area, the 77,000 square miles contaminated by the 1986 explosion at the Chernobyl Nuclear Power Plant in Ukraine. Among their findings there: reduced numbers and longevity of birds; diminished fertility in male birds; smaller brains in some birds; and mutations in swallows and other species that indicate significant genetic damage. Barn swallows and wood warblers, among other species, are locally extinct.

The shameful part is we haven't learned our lesson about the catastrophic consequences of nuclear radiation after Pennsylvania's Three Mile Island accident in 1979, Chernobyl in 1986 and Fukushima in 2011. Even worse, some of the nuclear plants have been built on known seismic regions. According to BBC reporter Greg Palast, reporter engineers knew Fukushima might be unsafe, but covered it up. Based on a first-hand interview by a senior engineer for the corporation which built the Fukushima nuclear plants, and a review of engineers' field diaries, it was revealed that the engineers who built the Fukushima nuclear plants knew their design would fail in an earthquake. Their report stated: the plant was riddled with problems that, no way on earth, could withstand an earthquake. The team of engineers sent in to inspect it found that most of these components could "completely and utterly fail" during an earthquake.

In 2004, Leuren Moret warned the Japan Times of the exact type of nuclear catastrophe that Japan experienced and said: "Of all the places in the entire world where no one in their right mind would build scores of nuclear power plants, Japan would be pretty near the top of the list."

Japan sits on top of four tectonic plates, at the edge of the subduction zone, and is in one of the most tectonically active regions of the world. "I think the situation right now is very scary," said Katsuhiko Ishibashi, a seismologist and professor at Kobe University. "It's like a kamikaze terrorist wrapped in bombs just waiting to explode."

Here's the kicker—for Earth's 7.2 billion inhabitants—radiation stays dangerous forever, or as long as humans are likely to exist, but the most dangerous parts will have decayed to only a small proportion of their original activity after a few thousand years. I'm afraid that if we don't hurry and find alternative sources of energy that won't harm our planet and the environment, we are headed in for extinction. There is solar energy, wind energy, water energy and yet not enough is being done. I've often thought that the planet Mars was a reminder to us Earthlings that an advanced civilization once existed there but destroyed their planet as we seem destined to do if we remain on the same destructive path.

Ocean Acidification

You probably haven't heard about this because our mainstream news isn't reporting on it—it's call ocean acidification which is increasing at an unprecedented rate. As humanity continues to fill the atmosphere with harmful gases, our planet is becoming less hospitable to life. The vast oceans absorb much of the carbon dioxide we have produced from the Industrial Revolution.

Due to Earth absorbing 25 percent of humanity's CO_2, has spared the atmosphere severe consequences, according to some scientists. But in light of the extreme weather worldwide in the past few years that may no longer be true. However, the news media can't hide the climate weirding of hurricane superstorms, fierce tornado cells, disastrous snowstorms, and record-setting global high temperatures.

The rising carbon dioxide in our oceans burns up and deforms the smallest, most plentiful food at the bottom of the deep blue food chain. One such victim is the sea butterfly. In just a few short decades, the death and deformation of this fragile and translucent species could endanger larger species that rely on the sea butterfly for food. This "butterfly effect," could potentially threaten fisheries that feed more than 1 billion humans worldwide.

Computer modeler Isaac Kaplan at the National Oceanic and Atmospheric Administration off in Seattle said that his early work predicts significant declines in sharks, skates and rays, some types of flounder and sole and Pacific whiting, the most frequently caught commercial fish off the coasts of Washington, Oregon and California. The increase in carbon dioxide might have caused the huge die-off off sea stars from California to Alaska in recent years.

Once a species immune system is weakened, it's vulnerable to disease.

Acidification can even rewire the brains of fish. Studies have found rising CO_2 levels cause clown fish to gain athleticism, but have their sense of smell redirected. This transforms them into "dumb jocks," scientist claim, swimming faster and more vigorously straight into the mouths of their predators. These Frankenstein fish were found to be five times more likely to die in the natural world. Could this be a metaphor for humanity, as our recklessness and abuse of Earth propels us toward an equally dangerous fate.

Craig Welch from the Seattle Times and others have reported, carbon dioxide is changing the ocean's chemistry faster than at any time in human history, in ways that have potentially devastating consequences for both ocean life and for humans who depend on the world's fisheries as vital sources of protein and livelihood.

Fracking

Fracking, also known as hydraulic fracturing, is the process of extracting natural gas from shale rock layers deep within the Earth. Fracking makes it possible to produce natural gas extraction in shale that was once unreachable with conventional technologies.

Fracking involves drilling and injecting fluid into the ground at a high pressure in order to fracture shale rocks to release natural gas inside. It takes 1-8 million gallons of water to complete each fracturing job. The water brought in is mixed with sand and chemicals to create fracking fluid. This is hard to believe but approximately 40,000 gallons of chemicals are used per fracturing. Up to 600 chemicals are used in fracking fluid, including known highly toxic and carcinogenic materials such as uranium, mercury, ethytene glycol, methanol, hydrochloric acid and formaldehyde.

Around 10,000 feet the fracking fluid is then pressure injected into the ground through a drilled pipeline. The mixture reaches the end of the well where the high pressure causes the nearby shale rock to crack, creating fissures where *natural gas* flows into the well. During this process, *methane gas and toxic chemicals* leach out from the system and contaminate nearby groundwater.

Methane concentrations are seventeen times *higher* in drinking-water wells near fracturing sites than in normal wells.

This contaminated well water is used for drinking water for nearby cities and towns. There have been over 1,000 documented cases of water contamination next to areas of gas drilling as well as cases of sensory, respiratory, and neurological damage due to ingested contaminated water. In Bradford County, Pennsylvania methane gas, a highly flammable gas, has seeped into ground water from fracking. Residents there can actually light their water with a match from the methane gas now in their drinking water. Many people have moved now that methane gas pockets have formed under and around their homes.

The waste fluid from fracking is left in open air pits to evaporate, releasing harmful VOC's (volatile organic compounds) into the atmosphere, creating contaminated air, acid rain, and ground level ozone. In the end, hydraulic fracking produces approximately 300,000 barrels of natural gas a day, but at the price of numerous environmental, safety, and health hazards.

There are those who could argue that we need this oil and gas, and at the moment that is true, but at what price? Fracking is also blamed on the swarm earthquakes taking place in the United States. Evidence continues to mount that fracking for oil and gas has caused hundreds of swarm earthquakes in southwestern Oregon, Nevada, Texas, Oklahoma, Ohio and Kansas recently. These earthquakes might be linked to oil and gas fracking, but there could be something far greater happening. While the quakes are far more often tied to disposal of drilling waste, scientists also increasingly have started pointing to the fracking process itself. Oklahoma Geological Survey seismologist Austin Holland stated to his colleagues that this has been happening more than they previously recognized. Currently, there are 500,000 active gas wells in the United States.

I believe, like paranormal writers and indigenous people, that more than fracking is to blame for the swarm earthquakes—like deep core Earth movement.

We are removing the life blood of Mother Earth, and she is kicking back—fighting for her life. The oil and gas industries ignorance and abuse for our Mother Earth will have major consequences for us in the years to come—not only with earthquakes but the release of methane gas now bubbling up from the oceans and land. The release of methane gas might also be contributing to global warming, a highly debated topic.

Pesticides and Herbicides

Scientists are baffled by the collapse of bee colonies worldwide. Scientists have been trying to discover why millions of beehives have collapsed and died during the past six years. Dozens of different types of chemicals may be combining to wreak havoc on the pollen that the bees collect for their hives.

Do we ask too much of animals and insects while forcing them to work for us? Are they rebelling? Animals are very concerned with the quality of life—much more so than humans. When the quality of life is in question, the animals automatically migrate toward a more sustaining reality. They remove themselves into other domains of existence, for they are programmed to survive.

As I have written, animals are intelligent and flexible and have many more adventures than humans do. Animals don't need to build shopping malls, graveyards, watch television, text on cell phones, watch movies, and distract themselves with these forms of entertainment. Do you think animals get bored? Do you think animals ever wonder what to do? They have many, many adventures that you are not quite capable of understanding, though you will one day, and at night when they dream, they enter other realities.

Insects are represented in greater numbers than any other class of animals on your planet, and they take up less space. They keep a balance, for without the insects our planet could not exist. Insects are multidimensional and act as unseen guardians for many worlds.

As you demonstrate your acknowledgment of intelligence in all forms of life, you begin to qualify as an ambassador or diplomatic representative of these various species. Life will become very strange indeed.

In the coming years, a great number of us will be able to bring a magnificent new upliftment, a new way of being, and a new prayer to Earth Mother. Understand that there is great intelligence in all life forms, and the experience of all life is waiting for us in the *Library of Earth.*

Open your emotional selves and employ the vital force of love as key to your own spiritual evolution.

Dying Water

Around our planet, even in remote islands, our precious water is being polluted by pesticides and fertilizer that flow into the rivers and into the oceans, and this is creating a toxic blue-green algae, poisoning waters. Pesticides and fertilizers that run into rivers and then into the ocean are causing coral reef around the world to die, a process known as coral bleaching. The corals that form the structure of the great reef ecosystems of tropical seas depend upon a symbiotic relationship with algae-like unicellular protozoa that are photosynthetic within their tissues.

There is a fragile balance for the coral reefs of the world. The following can contribute to coral bleaching: herbicides, bacterial infections, cyanide fishing, silt runoff, mineral dust from African dust storms caused by drought and even sunscreen, non-biodegradable, washing off tourists swimming, snorkeling or diving.

Factories in the United States, China and throughout the world have toxic spills, and some of these toxins are intentionally dumped into rivers and lakes. In the documentary, *River of Waste,* the movie examines the potential hazards caused by factory farms in the United States, particularly by waste disposal. It shows how large-scale corporate farms use growth hormones that threaten human health and the future of our planet.

Some scientists have gone so far as to call the condemned current factory farm practices as *"mini Chernobyls."* In the U.S. and elsewhere, the meat and poultry industry is dominated by dangerous uses of arsenic, antibiotics, growth hormones and by the dumping of massive amounts of sewage in fragile waterways and environments. The film documents the vast catastrophic impact on the environment and public health as well as focuses on the individual lives damaged and destroyed.

Years ago, Western Shoshone spiritual leader Corbin Harney had a vision of our water becoming extremely polluted. Water spoke to him and said, *I'm going to look like water, but pretty soon nobody's going to use me.* In some places the water's already got chemicals in it, so much that they can't use it. And people are just continuing to put poison in that water.

"When I went to the coast, the ocean water there looked sad to me. The water is saying, *I need help.* Water talks like we do. It breathes air like we do. It's hard to believe, but it does. Everything drinks water, and everything's got a life to it."

Corbin wanted us to know that everything will suffer as our waters die. He believed that the redskin people had a change to survive because they are connected to what's out there. It is their prayers, he believed, that would help the water to continue to flow cleaner and purer.

Corbin was not a fatalist—he believed that if we unified in a common cause for the upliftment of Mother Earth, we could heal our waters and the entire planet, but it would take hard work and prayers to turn things around.

The Ancient Ones told humanity that is our job to care for Mother Earth's creatures and all the kingdoms of nature, according to the indigenous thirteen Grandmothers. In the creation myths handed down from generation to generation, it is said that in the beginning, wisdom and knowledge were gained from the animals, because the Creator did not speak to humans. The Ancient Ones observed all the kingdoms of nature—the stars, Grandfather Sun, Grandmother Moon. Everything on Earth has a purposed, they believed. For every disease, there is a plant spirit to cure it.

Grandmother Agnes Baker Pilgrim, world-renowned spiritual leader and Keeper of the Sacred Salmon Ceremony for her people, reminds us, "If we don't take care of our animal kingdom, we ourselves are dying faster than we think."

Grandmother Agnes Bake Pilgrim says, "We forget that everything comes from Mother Earth, even the clothes on our backs. We are in denial about what we are doing. We must see ourselves in the whole context. We all breathe the same air. Let's make it clean and healthy."

The Grandmothers tell us that the Ancient Ones, their ancestors, revered the Earth and used ritual and gratitude to sustain Earth's balance. It is important to reclaim that reverence and holiness. It is time to go back to appreciation and respect for Earth

Mother and all we have or there will be nothing left to appreciate. Every living thing on planet Earth has a reason to be here—it's the perfect order of the Universe. That is our spiritual lesson.

If you think you're too small to make a difference, try sleeping with a mosquito." —His Holiness The Dalai Lama

CHAPTER ELEVEN
Saving Earth

Often I'm asked the question how can one person save our planet? One person can accomplish wonders and miracles and it all starts with one person—You! One person can turn into hundreds, then thousands, and then millions. If each person takes responsibility for their lives to live a loving and compassionate life, that light of energy expands out and continues to grow. There is this physics concept called, *The Butterfly Effect,* which states a single butterfly flapping its wings on one side of the globe can, in theory, start a hurricane on the other side. In other words—we are connected to everything and everything is connected to us, and we affect each other in ways we can't even imagine. So, if a single butterfly flapping its wings can create a hurricane on the other side globe, just think what humans can do if we come together *en masse* to pray, visualize, intend, and dream a new world into existence.

The Earth warriors are people who are dedicated to healing our planet—and they are making a difference now. They are speaking up, peacefully protesting and making themselves known; speaking up that they've had enough of big corporations destroying Mother Earth with their greed. People like Erin Brockovich, a legal clerk and environmental activist, showed us how one person can make a difference in the hit 2000 movie, *Erin Brockovich*, starring Julia Roberts. It proved that a David of the world can conquer a Goliath, no matter how big and powerful. All it takes is persistence and faith.

The movie was based on the true story on how Erin built a case against the Pacific Gas and Electric Company (PG&E) of California in 1993, where the town of Hinkley, California's drinking water had become polluted by hexavalent chromium, a cancer-causing toxin. Many of the town's residents had cancer or had died of various cancers. Everything was against Erin and Edward Masry's law firm, where she was employed, but Erin believed she could fight Goliath (PG&E) and win. Erin and Edward's Masry's law firm won the case for the residents of Hinkley. The case was settled in 1996 for $333 million, the largest settlement ever paid in a direct-action lawsuit in U.S. history. Despite a formal education in law, Erin brought a case against PG & E, and won, proving one person can accomplish the impossible!

In the AARP October/November 2014 issue, environmental activist Erin Brockovich said, "Destroying the environment, deceiving people, jeopardizing their health and their welfare, is absolutely wrong. And if you wanna corner them, you're gonna corner me. And I come out swingin."

So you see, a mosquito can make a different in the world!

Since humans first emerged on planet Earth there have always been two types of beings: the Earthkeepers—those who find everything on Mother Earth unique and beautiful and walk upon her in a sacred manner, and those who set out to conquer and destroy everything in their path. Nothing has changed in eons.

Alberto Villoldo, Ph.D., a medical anthropologist who comes from a long line of Earthkeepers from the Amazon and the Andes, wrote in his book, *The Four Insights,* that the Laika people know that we can change our world as long as we are willing to take on karma. There is serpent karma where we try to change things by force; jaguar karma where we change things through will; hummingbird karma where we change events through visualization; and lastly, there is eagle karma, where we change things by dream.

At the level of serpent, karma is very slow, which is why some people seem to get away with terrible things. At jaguar level, karma is experienced a little faster, and always in this lifetime, and with hummingbird, karma is instant: both good deeds and bad actions. And with eagle, there is no karma, because there is only Spirit and "may Thy will be done."

When we realize that we're dreaming the world into being each minute, we recognize that we also create the nightmares of our reality. So why do we dream up such horrible nightmares and events? Because of mind and ego. The only way to create a world of peace and harmony is shut off mind.

An excellent analogy of this thought is the story Villoldo related in his book when he was hiking through the Altiplano with shaman don Antonio years ago and arrived at a village where it hadn't rained for many months. The villagers asked his mentor to call the rains. The old Laika asked for a hut where he fasted and meditated for four days, drinking only water. On the fourth day don Antonio emerged from the hut and walked to the edge of the village where the mountains began a drop to the Amazon basin, and told Villoldo he was going to "pray rain." Villoldo thought he misspoke and said, "You mean you are going to pray for rain."

The shaman replied, "No, I am going to pray rain."

At that instant, Villoldo understood what his teacher meant. He stepped into eagle, and dissolved. He had ceased to exist for that instant, and go into infinity. Only Spirit existed there—he simply prayed rain, and it rained.

Later Villoldo asked his mentor why it had taken so long to create rain and he answered that when he arrived at the village, he noticed that it was out of *ayni*. It was so out-of-balance, that he became out-of-balance, too. He couldn't create the rain until he went back into *ayni,* and when he did, so did the village, and the rains came. He knew that everything is healed from within.

Certainly, this is a lesson that could be applied to our entire planet. At this moment in time our planet is out-of-balance and so are we. In order to heal our world we must get in balance, *in ayni,* the proper relationship of everything. As soon as we awaken to the fact we are dreaming the world into existence, our nightmares will end.

When it comes to Mother Earth, we are our Mother's keepers. Each and every one of us has a role to help heal our planet and right the wrong that has been done to her in the last one-hundred plus years. Whether you believe that disastrous Earth changes and severe weather taking place now are natural processes or one created by humans, or both, the fact is we are seeing our ice caps melt at an unprecedented rate, sea levels are rising and severe weather patterns that include drought, tornadoes, hurricanes, tsunamis, and flash floods, have become the norm. These are the signs spoken of by the indigenous people worldwide who say that the Star being are guiding them and warning them to be prepared.

I've included ways you can make a difference by practicing *Earth Wisdom* to the highest degree.

Cosmetics, Personal Care Products and Hair Dyes

We all use shampoos, mouthwash, laundry soap, lotions, skin cleansers, bubble bath, stain remover, suntan lotion, pet shampoos, toothpastes, soaps, and dish detergents that contain toxic substances like sodium laureth sulfate (SLES) and acrylates copolymer. Both *Sodium Laureth Sulfate* (SLES) and its close relative Sodium Lauryl Sulfate (SLS) cause the product to "foam up." Both chemicals are very effective foaming agents, chemically known as surfactants.

Although sodium laureth sulfate is somewhat less irritating than SLS, it cannot be metabolized by the liver and its effects are therefore much longer-lasting. This not only means it stays in the body tissues for longer, but much more precious energy is used getting rid of it.

Shampoos are among the most frequently reported products to the FDA. Reports include eye irritation, scalp irritation, tangled hair, swelling of the hands, face and arms and split and fuzzy hair. This is highly characteristic of sodium laureth sulfate and almost definitely directly related to its use. These products may have long-lasting side effect for children.

So why is a dangerous chemical like sodium laureth sulfate used in our soaps and shampoos?

The answer is simple—it is cheap. The sodium laureth sulfate found in our soaps is exactly the same as you would find in a car wash or even a garage, where it is used to degrease car engines. Although the health implications are not fully known, the additive may be responsible for health problems ranging from PMS to menopausal systems in women to dropping male fertility and autism in children. It can also be related to female cancers such as breast cancer, where oestrogen levels are known to be involved.

Is it any wonder cancer and autism is so prevalent in young children? What to do? Buy natural products that don't contain added laureth sulfate which you can purchase at health food and organic stores. When you stop buying these products, it sends a clear message to the companies that you won't buy their product, and they will change their products. Remember when the Coca Cola Company tried to the New Coke in 1985 and changed the original formula? There was such a huge backlash that they took it off the market and returned to the Classic Coke.

Did you know that Crest recently introduced a 3D White toothpaste containing polyethylene plastic beads? Dentists and hygienists have removed plastic beads from the gums of their patients. This is pure insanity by corporations that care little about our well-being. I suspect all these products are linked to the increase of Alzheimer's disease, dementia in the elderly, autism in children and cancers in children and adults. All you have to do is listen to drug commercials on television to learn about the horrible side effects prescription drugs can have on the human body.

Hair Dyes

I, like millions of women worldwide, use hair dye. Have you ever considered its toxicity? Consider this: how can something that smells so toxic be safe? The FDA has no authority to require that cosmetics be tested for safety before they are sold, unlike drugs and food additives. An industry-funded panel, not a government health agency, reviewed the safety of cosmetic ingredients in the

U.S. Research undertaken by Environmental Working Group (EWG) showed that this largely self-regulated industry routinely failed to adhere to their own safety panel's advice or to heed the health warnings inherent in cosmetic safety standards set in other countries.

In an investigation of the ingredients in more than 23,000 hair and cosmetics products, EWG found that nearly one of every 30 products sold in the U.S. fails to meet one or more industry or governmental cosmetics safety standards. They also found nearly 40 products sold in the U.S. contain chemicals that are prohibited for use in cosmetics in other countries, and over 400 products containing ingredients that cosmetic industry safety panels have found unsafe when used as directed on product labels, including the U.S. based Cosmetic Ingredient Review (CIR) and the International Fragrance Association.

You as a consumer can familiarize yourself with ingredients banned by the European Commission, and check the label of products you use or consider using. Think natural if possible! I know it's hard to resist the hair color, but think how you will be healing Mother Earth of toxic substances that go right back into ground and water.

What's So Great About Organic?

- Organic is grown and processed without synthetic pesticides, herbicides and GMOs.
- Organic is preservative free—no nitrates or sulfates.
- With organic there's less soil erosion.
- Lee groundwater pollution.
- Lastly, with organic produce the soil is enriched and drought resistant.

GMOs

Genetically modified organisms or foods (GMO foods) have been shown to cause harm to humans, animals, and the environment, and despite growing opposition, more and more foods continue to be genetically altered—biotech giant Monsanto is one of the worst offenders. It may be difficult to completely avoid GMOs, and you should merely try to find other sources other than your big chain grocer. If produce is certified USDA-organic, it's non-GMO (or supposed to be!). Also, seek out local farmers and booths at farmer's markets where you can be ensured that the crops aren't GMO. Even better, if you are so inclined: start your own organic garden.

GMO Foods to Avoid

Soy in all forms is GMO unless its organic—tofu, soy sauce, soy oil, and most products including salad dressings, herbal teas, packaged food products, and even your vitamins contain GMO.

Corn and corn products, sugar beets have been genetically altered as well, and even papayas grown in Hawaii, zucchini and yellow squash. Canola oil has been chemically altered. The dangers of these GMO foods are well-known. The Bt toxin being used in GMO corn, for example, was recently detected in the blood of pregnant women and their babies. But perhaps more frightening are the risks that are still *unknown*.

Beware of artificial sweeteners and their known side effects. Aspartame is a toxic additive sweetener created with a genetically-altered bacteria. Splenda is also suspected of harmful side effects.

Plastics:

Recycle plastics, cardboard, and glass. Urge your local companies, restaurants, cities and parks to place recycle receptacles for plastics inside stores, offices and city parks.

Plastics are both a miracle and a curse in our modern world. In the medical world plastic has been lifesaving for millions of people, but on the other hand plastic is everywhere and it takes thousands of years for it to breakdown. The toxins in plastic containers seep into our water, various foods and beverages. We use billions of plastic bags to store food and dump our trash, but I remember a time before plastics when we used biodegradable paper bags for our trash cans supplied by grocery stores.

So next time you go to grocery store, bring your cloth bag and forget the plastic bag. Just say NO to plastic!

With 7.2 billion humans on the planet now and growing, we produce mega tons of trash each day that goes into landfills and into our waters. It is estimated that eight million tons of plastic enters the ocean waters every year. We, as contributing individuals, have the responsibility to help clean up our ecosystem, not only for the sake of our environment, but for our own health and survival. By using Earth-friendly shopping bags at the grocery store to recycling, and even speaking up will make a huge difference in our world.

Before the days of plastic when fishermen dumped their trash overboard or lost a net, it consisted of natural materials like rope, cloth, paper and some metal that would either sink to the bottom or biodegrade quickly. But plastic remains floating on the surface of the oceans, the same place where many genuine food sources lie-- and can remain so for 400 years or more. Plastic is durable and strong—precisely the quality that make it so dangerous if it reaches the waters of our world.

About 20 percent of the plastic in the oceans comes from ships or offshore platforms; the rest is blown, washed off the land or intentionally dumped. Unless removed, plastics will remain in the sea for hundreds of years, breaking up into ever-smaller particles. Recently, scientists discovered that miscroscopic pieces of plastic can be found everywhere in the oceans, even inside plankton, the keystone of the marine food chain. It's killing our marine life.

Buy glass whenever you can to escape the addiction for plastic. We lived without plastic for thousands of years and we can do it now! Swap up for a greener options. Instead of buying more plastic wrap, plastic containers, and tin foil, purchase glass containers.

The Waste in Our Landfills

In the January 21, 2015 issue of Boise, Idaho Weekly, George Prentice made a startling discovery about Ada County's landfill. He discovered that tons of edible food like vegetables, fruit, bread, meat, pasta, cheese—that appear edible, or was at least edible when it was discarded was thrown away because of the expiration date or sell-by date, placed on the product. The sell-by date is for the store owner and the use-by date is for the consumer. For some strange reason people are convinced that the product has to be thrown away on that date even when the product is still edible.

This is one of a number of startling discoveries in the analysis prepared for Ada County by South Prairie, Washington based Green Solutions, LLC. From yard debris to massive amounts of recyclable wood and carpeting were found in Ada County's landfill. People forget that yard debris and food waste can be used for composting.

It was estimated that 33,280 tons of construction and/or demolition materials pile up annually. Even more stunning it is estimated that approximately 80 percent of (C & D) waste, including plywood, carpeting and roofing, is potentially recyclable.

Cleaning Supplies

Replace your toxic household cleaners and detergents with products that say they are biodegradable or safe for the environment. You don't have to spend a lot on natural cleaning products—think vinegar, lemon water and baking soda—excellent natural cleaning products. Dump the bleach powered cleansers for baking soda—it's natural and safe.

Mercury Light Bulbs vs Incandescent Light Bulbs

There are pros and cons for both. Compact fluorescent light bulbs are one of the easiest ways to shrink your power bill and your carbon footprint. They help the environment, but there's the higher retail price. They last up to 10 times longer than incandescent bulbs, which mean you get a great savings. CFLs use only 104 kilowatts of electricity compared to 480 kilowatts with an Incandescent bulb.

The biggest negative against CFLs is their toxic content. There's a small amount of toxic mercury in everyone one of them if broken, which can be absorbed or inhaled, potentially causing brain damage in adults, children and fetuses. Break a CFL while changing a light, critics warn, and you unleash a poisonous hazard in your home. And throwing them out and you're dumping mercury in landfills and into the Earth, and that toxic mercury can seep into our rivers, lakes, wells and our deep water aquifers.

For me, I'd rather use incandescent bulbs.

Swap for Greener Options

Replenish cleaning supplies with products that have the Environmental Protection Agency's logo or an environmental label. Eco-friendly claims can be misleading. Beware of labels that says "all-natural" or "friendly to the environment" which means the product doesn't have any specifics to back up the claim. Look for a seal indicating that the product has been certified green by a reputable their party, and then check with the certifier to ensure that the product really has been given the seal of approval. If the product is green but in a plastic container then you're not practicing green-living. Stay clear of foods with corn syrup or high fructose corn syrup, sulfites and nitrates. These additives are harmful.

Buy local, and support your local organic farmers and ranchers.

Hybrid Cars and the Bicycle

Need a new car, consider a hybrid car or ride a bike to work if you live close to work. Besides getting in shape, you will keep the oil and gas pollution down in your area.

Buy Organic Beauty Products

Here again, beauty products, many of them have been tested on animals. They can contain chemicals, pesticides, synthetic hormones and genetically modified organisms. Opt for organic shampoo, lotions, and make-up.

Ladies can you live without your fake nails and all the toxic chemicals used on your nails? Again, why not think natural. Expand your thinking to include organic in cosmetics, beauty produces, cleaning products, pet foods, clothing, vegetables, fruit, meat, fish and more.

Go Paperless

Today you can print newspaper and magazine subscriptions online. Use cloth napkins and clean up spills with a cloth towel or rags. Opt out of Direct Marketing and all the bulk mail by going to www.the-dma.org/consumers/offmailinglist. Opt out of mailed credit card offers by calling 888-567-8688 or logging on to www.optoutprescreen.com.

The trees of the world will thank you for your thoughtfulness and concern.

Did you know that approximately 5 million tons of disposable diapers contribute to U.S. landfills every year. I grew up in the fifties and sixties when mothers used cloth diapers. It wasn't easy to clean them, but that generation of mothers didn't pollute the planet with millions of tons of plastic diapers.

Disposable diapers contain polypropylene and wood-pulp fibers and can take as long as 500 years to decompose in a landfill. When you consider that most diaper services charge 7 cents to 11 cents per diaper, compared with 13 cents to 31 cents for disposables, doesn't it make perfect sense to use these services and help the planet?

Saving Water

Pure water everywhere is vanishing at an unprecedented rate. There are more than 783 million people who don't have access to clean water, a fact highlighted by the UN recently. There's three water vampires we use daily—toilets, showers, and the worst of all—dishwashers and clothes washers. By washing dishes by hand, flushing only when you need to and by connecting water saving shower heads you will save gallons of precious water.

Do you really need to run that dishwasher all the time? Do you really need to wash your car or RV at home instead of going to a car wash that recycles water? Did you know that a dishwasher uses 5.8 to 7 gallons of water per cycle? Burn some calories and wash your dishes by hand once in a while and save some water. Just think if millions of us tried this and the water and energy we'd save.

More than 45% of water use in the average American home occurs in the bathroom, with nearly 27% being used by toilets. You can significantly curb toilet water usage by regularly checking for and fixing leaks, retrofitting older toilets, or installing a new toilet, but also make sure that your toilet tank doesn't fill to the top.

There are people trying to remedy our water crisis. One such person is an eccentric genius, Dean Kamen, known for his Segway invention. Kamen invented the SlingShot, an energy-efficient machine that turns any unfit water (seawater, poisoned wells, river sludge) into pure, safe water—no chemicals or filters needed, by means of vapor compression distillation. It can be operated by using cow dung as fuel. Recently Kamen partnered with the Coca-Cola Company to place his machines throughout developing nations in Africa and Central America in hopes of eliminating the millions of deaths each year related to waterborne disease.

Currently, more than 1 billion people throughout the world have no access to safe water. It is reported that 4,900 children under the age of 5 die per day due to water and sanitation problems. In third-world countries, dirty water is a greater threat to human safety than violence. It is now estimated that by 2025, close to 3 billion people will live in water scare regions of the world.

Saving Trees

Each year it is estimated that over 34 million trees are cut down for holiday Christmas trees around the world. I realize that tree farms specifically grow trees for Christmas decoration—but why not buy a living tree to be planted after the holidays? Large cities cut down tall pine trees to decorate for the holiday season, a senseless act, I believe. Again, why not find a large living tree to decorate and replant.

Check out the Reforest'Action, an environmental organization that plants trees worldwide, in the areas where they're needed most.

Saving Wildlife

There are poachers on every continent that kill for the sport of it, and not for food or survival. In Africa, elephants and rhinos are slaughtered for their tusks and sold in Asian countries, and in Central Africa gorillas and chips are killed for bush meat and being pushed to extinction because of an appetite for luxury food and virgin timber. Unrestrained logging, mostly by European companies driving new access roads into old-growth forests, makes the proliferation possible. Roads now penetrate deep into areas once inaccessible to hunters.

Also gorillas are killed for their hands which are made into ashtrays and sold to tourists or anyone willing to buy them. Other parts of the body are also sold for profit. The problem is that the poachers that do this are uneducated and extremely poor. There are few programs to educate the people on the harm they are doing to an already fragile ecosystem. Also mountain gorilla infants are abducted for illegal selling to zoos and as pets. This often results in other adult gorillas being killed in the process.

Thankfully, there are organizations like (NWF) National Wildlife Federation that helps to protect wildlife and inspire future generations. The NWF is dedicated to protecting wildlife by:

- Helping Wildlife in a Warming World
- Safeguarding Endangered Species
- Stopping the Spread of Invasive Species
- Building Corridors for Wildlife
- Implementing State Wildlife Action Plans
- Restoring Wild Bison to the Great Plains
- Advancing Red Wolf Recovery
- Stopping Carbon Pollution
- Reducing Harmful Drilling and Mining
- Advocating for Renewable Energy
- Promoting Clean Transportation
- Stopping Deforestation
- Helping Wildlife in a Warming World

Save Electricity
Do you really need all the lights on in the house? Turn off those lights when you are not in a room and cut down on your electric bill and consumption of energy. Lower the temperature during the winter, and during the summer, use less air conditioning by setting the thermostat higher.

Honor Yourself
Mother Earth gives to us food, water, and oxygen. But we need to reciprocate her generosity by honoring and respecting her and ourselves. We mirror Earth and she mirrors us. If we don't take care of ourselves, Earth in her intuitive way feels our negative energy. Being an Earthkeeper means loving yourself and your body first by eating wholesome and organic foods and staying free

of toxic substances, such as recreational drugs, large amounts of alcohol, and prescribed drugs. If you stay healthy, and eat properly, you will find you don't require all the pharmaceutical drugs on the market that promise to alleviate your symptom but cause a harmful side effect. What you do to your body, your sacred temple, you do to Mother Earth. Remember the substances you put into your body, go directly into the water and into the soil.

Fluoride Toothpaste

Fluoride toothpaste fights cavities but it could cause health problems. It's been known since the very early 1950's that ingestion of fluoride could cause mental retardation. Fluoride is a naturally occurring mineral. Though it's not an essential nutrient it is present in many foods. However, today we are exposed to fluorides from a wide range of sources, including air pollution, drinking water, toothpaste, mouth rinses, beverages, medicines, anesthetics, fluoride supplements, pesticides and herbicide residues.

For most of us our main exposure to it is through our water supply and through toothpaste and mouth washes. Unlike chlorine, which is added to our water for purposes of disinfection, fluoride is added to drinking water as a forced medication (to prevent tooth decay). In fact, fluoride is the only chemical added to water for this purpose.

Like so many everyday substances that have been found to be toxic, fluoride has its roots in World War II research into weapons of mass destruction. Massive quantities of fluoride were essential for the manufacture of bomb-grade uranium and plutonium for nuclear weapons throughout the Cold War.

Post WWII, fluoride was a popular form of rat poison. However, as fluoride production began to greatly outstrip its use as a rodenticide, scientists were spurred on by industry and the government to find other uses for it.

Today, fluoride is routinely added to the water supply of around 10% of the UK population (though this figure is set to rise) and more than 60% of the US population. These figures are in stark contrast to the 98% of Western Europe that has rejected fluoridation because it doesn't work and that it is morally reprehensible to forcibly medicate whole populations of people.

Deceptive Labeling on Foods

Many of our foods today are imported from China and other Asian countries. The labeling may not tell you it's made in a foreign country like China, but instead it might read: "distributed by" with the name of a U.S. company. That means that United States distributor imported the product and only shipped it across the country to grocery retailers and pet stores. If it doesn't say made in **USA**, it's not!

Many pet treats and pet foods are made in China. Beware—these products often contain poisonous ingredients. The FDA linked illnesses from Chinese jerky products to 3,600 dogs and 10 cats since 2007 in all 50 U.S. states and six Canadian provinces. It is estimated over 600 dogs died from these toxic products and an unknown number of cats.

Grow Your Own Garden

Buy from local organic growers or grow your own garden. Recycling vegetable scraps is a great way to compost your garden. In Oprah's Magazine June 2013 issue, Oprah decided to create a farm on Maui. So she teamed up with her friend Bob Greene to create a garden in the rich soil of Hawaii. What shocked me was that Hawaii, even with their rich red soil, about 90 percent of the food on the island is flown or shipped in from other places, which makes it expensive to buy—not to mention the carbon footprint involved in getting it to Maui.

Oprah and Bob wanted to give back to the land and Maui, so they designated 16 acres for farming. In 2012 with the help of a natural-resource management group, Bio-Logical Capital, they planted a singled acre with more than 100 species of fruits, vegetables, and herbs. They discovered which crops would thrive there.

Bob had known that our modern-day health issues stem from the fact that so much of the food we eat, especially processed foods, lack in essential nutrients that they used to have due in part to soil being depleted from pesticides and over-farming. Our bodies are starved for real nutrients in fruits and vegetables that vitamin supplements can equal. Have you noticed most vegetables are tasteless, especially those found in most grocery stores (non-organic)?

Although Bob assumed the Maui soil was full of nutrients, he discovered it needed help and again Bio-Logical Capital came to the rescue. They recycled edible scraps from fruits and vegetables, compost from organic material like leaves, plant clippings and grass clippings and added fertilizer from the chicken coop (cow manure could have been used as well). To avoid damaging the soil with pesticides, Oprah's team relied on confusing pests: never plant the same crop in the same spot two seasons in a row. This forces insect pests to work harder to find the crops they like.

The farm produced 145 pounds of food each week and much of it was given to locals. Oprah said the experience of a farm gave her a greater appreciation of the food she puts into her body.

In the past few years my husband and I have planted a small garden in our southwestern Idaho home. Our garden usually consists of kale, zucchini, squash, eggplant, a variety of tomatoes and always lots of herbs like mint, rosemary and basil. It's such an exhilarating feeling touching Mother Earth and smelling her earthiness, and then watching the tiny sprouts poke their heads from the ground. Each day I'd say a prayer over our garden and thank the life for its bounty. Even my insect friends are thanked—lady bugs, praying mantis, dragonflies, butterflies and honey bees for doing their amazing part as keepers of the garden. There are also invisible spirits that watch over our gardens and should be thanked.

Cows the Natural Way

I found a fascinating article by Heather Pratt, MNT in Natural Grocers magazine, May 2014, and thought, wow, someone is thinking outside the box when it comes to balancing our planet and reversing climate change. She says we should eat more pastured beef and dairy; for those not vegetarians. This may be a big environmental remedy, and here's why: scientists and researchers say that greenhouse gases are creating climate change, and they are referring to carbon dioxide, although other gases such as methane and nitrous oxide, also contribute. These gases create a greenhouse effect that traps the sun's heat in the atmosphere. To some extent this is good because it warms the Earth enough to sustain life; however, when there is an excess of these gases in the atmosphere, too much heat is trapped and this excess heat alters weather patterns.

Plants pull carbon dioxide out of the atmosphere and store it in a stable form in the soil, where it promotes fertility, mains beneficial microbes, and improves the soils ability to hold water, which helps it resist both floods and drought.

When in balance, the release of gases into the atmosphere is countered by gases being absorbed and stored in the soil. However, when humans began modern building and agricultural practices (a process called desertification), that perfect balance was lost. So if we focus on reducing the amount of gases released in the atmosphere it will certainly slow climate change—it's really our best hope.

Think pastured cows, not cows raised in confinement dairies in indoor barns or in dirt yards piled in manure. This isn't humane or natural for cows. Confinement dairies are far removed from the cute little cow grassing on green pastures pictured on your carton of milk. Most of these cows are fed GMO corn or soy and require large amount of drugs to keep up high production rates in order to counter the illnesses that are so prevalent in these operations.

Pastured cows can affect climate change. First we must get away from raising cattle in confined feedlots and pens. Nearly 97 percent of the beef eaten in the United States are raised in feedlots. Raising conventional beef in Concentrated Animal Feeding Operations (CAFOs) burdens the environment. In CAFOs cows are fattened quickly on a steady diet of grains, mostly GMO corn. This corn requires large amounts of synthetic nitrogen-based fertilizers, which are produced using large amounts of fossil fuels. It takes approximately 100 gallons of oil to grow enough corn to raise a single cow.

Corn crops in the United States have also converted large areas of fertile grasslands into virtual deserts that lie barren outside of the growing season, and aren't much better in regard to soil health even when crops are growing. And then there's the waste: when thousands of cattle are raised in tight quarters there is a lot of manure to deal with. Many CAFOs rely on manmade ponds or other structures for storing manure, which can pollute rivers and underground drinking water when not properly managed. Stored in this liquid form, manure also contributes to greenhouse gases in the atmosphere. The current method of raising cattle is not only unsustainable; it's harming the environment and the planet.

So you are probably asking how cattle raised on pasture land can be so different. First of all, pastured cattle don't require much supplemental feed because they spend their time outdoors grazing on grass. Thousands of cows are not crowded into one small space and stressed like CAFOs, which means less water and air pollution. But there's more—this type of ranching restores the soil's ability to absorb and store greenhouse gases. Cows, and other types of ruminants like sheep, goats, bison, elk, and deer, have a unique symbiotic relationship with the land. All these animals move as they graze, most likely to avoid predators, which prevents overgrazing. This pattern of movement also encourages the restoration of the soil. They contribute fertilizer to the soil in the form of manure and then the manure acts as a food to beneficial microbes and delivers more of those microbes to the soil.

Also, their hooves work the land by helping decompose dead matter into the soil, thus spreading seeds for germination. This all makes the soil healthier and leads to more plant growth, and in turn the soil absorbs more and stores greenhouse gases from the atmosphere. This is natural doing what it does best.

What about methane, a potent greenhouse gas that cattle expel? Here's the amazing part of about free-grazing cattle, they emit nearly 20 percent less methane gas compared to their conventional counterparts. Additionally, through their manure, ruminants contribute microbes to the soil that have the ability to absorb methane from the air and break it down thus offsetting their methane "emissions." CAFO cattle cause a greater gas problem for Earth.

Next time you buy beef look for the certified grassfed labels: Food Alliance Certified Grass-fed, the American Grass-fed Association, or USDA verified grass-fed, all of which require that the cattle eat a diet exclusively of forage their entire lives. Labels can also include: "100% grass-fed" or "grass finished."

Buying dairy products (butter, yogurt, cheese, etc.) which

allow chicken, turkey, lamb, pork and beef to feed on grass will contribute to a healthy environment and stop animal abuse in cages and confined pens.

The Ag-Gag Law

Recently, Idaho, Utah, Iowa and several other states have passed what has become known as the Ag-Gag law. Idaho's Governor C.L. "Butch" Otter signed a bill February 2014 that imposes jail time and fines against people who secretly film animal abuse in Idaho's agricultural facilities. The bill came in response to videos released by Los Angeles-based vegetarian and animals rights group Mercy for Animals which showed workers at the Bettencourt Dairy in Jerome, Idaho beating, stomping, dragging and sexually abusing dairy cows in 2012.

Idaho's $2.5 billion dairy industry complained the group used its videos not to curb abuse, but to unfairly hurt Bettencourt's business, which owns more than 60,000 cows and is one of the largest dairy companies in the United States.

Now if an animal of any kind is abused, the abusers can get away with it. The activists, if caught, can get up to one year in prison and fined up to a thousand dollars. Why don't animals have rights? Reporters have noted that some of these laws (in particular, Pennsylvania's bill) could also be used to criminalize anti-fracking activists, or those who protest the drilling of shale oil and gas using hydraulic fracturing or "fracking" technique.

A few years ago I tried to report the abuse of several horses kept in a small fenced area, standing in deep cold mud for days on end. I called the Humane Society who said they didn't handle large livestock and referred me to an agricultural agency. They said there had been a great number of complaints against the owner of the horses, but they couldn't get close to his farm without owner's permission. So nothing was done! It angers me there is an idiotic bureaucracy in certain states that allow domestic animals to be abused, because an owner has rights, but not the animals.

How can we start to heal Mother Earth if we have no respect for the animals that enrich our lives and feed us? When these businesses think they can get away with abuse, they need to think again. There is karma to be paid on the physical side and the spiritual side. We are all part of the "Great Mystery" as Native Americans refer to our Creator, and all life has the right to be treated kindly with honor and respect. We are all related to all things on Mother Earth.

When we begin to understand the divinity, the cosmology of all life, we will no longer take our beautiful planet for granted. In these days, when the prophecies are being fulfilled, we are the ones who will determine whether or not we will destroy Mother Earth and ourselves. —The 13 Indigenous Grandmothers

CHAPTER TWELVE
Earth Wisdom

From October 11 through October 17, 2004 something extraordinary happened when the Thirteen Indigenous Grandmothers met for the first time in Phoenicia, New York. They traveled from the Amazon rain forest, the Arctic circle of North America, the great forests of the American Northwest, the vast plains of North America, the highlands of Central America, the

Black Hills of South Dakota, the mountains of Oaxaca, Mexico, the American Southwest, the mountains of Tibet, and the rain forest of central Africa.

Their calling was for a common vision to form a new global alliance with traditional medicine people and communities throughout the world. They united in New York as one in prayer, education and healing for Mother Earth and all her inhabitants, for the children of the world and the next seven generations.

Their urgency was for the abuse and disregard of Mother Earth—the unprecedented destruction of the air, waters, and soil; the atrocities of war, the global scourge of poverty; the threat of nuclear weapons and waste permeating the planet; the prevailing culture of materialism; the epidemics that threaten the health of Earth's peoples; the exploitation of indigenous medicines; and the destruction of the indigenous culture and knowledge handed down from generation to generation.

The Grandmothers believe that their ancestral wisdom of prayer, ceremony, peacemaking and healing are urgently needed now. In the beautifully written book, *Grandmothers Counsel the World—Women Elders Offer their Vision of Our Planet,* author Carol Schaefer interviewed each of the Thirteen Indigenous Grandmothers. The wisdom and guidance they imparted is invaluable to us and the steps we must take to insure that future generations have a thriving and healthy planet.

Grandmother Clara of the Amazon was visited by the Star Beings, and on 12-21-2012, she was told that this event heralded the "Galactic Dawn"—a mass awakening of humanity to our cosmic origins and intergalactic relationships. "What I see today in the world is a lot of darkness and a few points of light trying to illuminate us as we go through the dark tunnel of our Age. We Grandmothers here are holding each other's hands, illuminating the path, so that we can bring health to this Mother Earth and heal the wounds. She is suffering from wounds made by ignorant men, ignorant of the truth of the Light and of the Creator. The message from the Beings of the Stars is that it is necessary for everyone to open their hearts to the truth of the Spirit, of the Spirit World, as it is this truth that will lead us to our salvation," says Grandmother Clara.

As the Earth changes accelerate each year—extreme weather,

increased earthquakes and volcanic activity worldwide, and sinkholes forming everywhere, we are moving into a time of cleansing of accumulated negativity caused by humanity's greed and materialism. We are out of balance say the Grandmothers, but Earth's changes will bring about an awakening of spiritual consciousness in humanity. There is the possibility of a great number of people leaving the planet. During times of crisis, people help each other—that's where the real spirit of humanity shines.

All the Grandmothers agree we must develop a different relationship with Mother Earth, or humanity will find themselves in a dire predicament. They say people will need physical, mental, emotional and spiritual strength to change; otherwise a huge portion of the population will suffer immeasurably. Unfortunately, at this time, most of humanity is materially oriented instead of spiritually oriented.

Napalese Grandmother Aama Bombo called upon Kali, the female goddess who can take the form of the Destroyer, during her prayer with the Grandmothers in New Mexico. Aama conveyed: "Kali is not happy with what is going on in the world. She sees that humanity is lacking in good values, and she is not happy with the cruelty of the people, who have been killing each other every day just to fulfill their selfish egos. They are poisoning the Motherland and the sky. This has led to the suffocation of all the creatures, who are not allowed a fresh breath. Spirituality and its values have been subordinated to the ego and to injustice."

The Grandmothers say we must learn love and compassion again. The people who will survive are those who love and affirm life in every way. But we must be willing to change the way we view the living library of Earth—all creation. The survivors will be those who are open to a whole new level of consciousness and seek true communication with the Earth and Creator.

Grandmother Flordemayo says the Maya are among those whose prophecy reveals a new consciousness coming where the feminine will prevail again. "I come from the Star People of the Pleiades, and I am also a child of Central America. In our oral teachings, we were told that at this particular time it will be the women who lead the nations. I bow to the spirit of women from the beginning of time, the spirit of woman that is within all of us. Male/female, female/male—we all come from that One. We are also told that at this time it is the energy of the stars that will move the nations."

Grandmother Mona believes the Hopi legend of the butterfly can help us through turbulent times of darkness and confusion by revealing to us our path of transformation. These times are necessary for learn and enabling humanity as a whole to transform into comprehension of the truth of our oneness with each other and with all of Creation. Only by going into darkness and breaking down the old ways can we move from the myopic view of the caterpillar to the greatly expanded view of the butterfly—the only way we will save our planet for the next generations to come.

Yupik Grandmother Rita Blumenstein explains that with every new experience, we have the power to redefine ourselves, so that no matter what our past mistakes, we can always change. "The past is not a burden. It is a scaffold which has brought us to this day. With this understanding, we are free to be who we are. We create our lives out of our past and out of the present. The quicker way to heal is by going forward, however—not by spending a great amount of time and energy dwelling on the past. We are our ancestors when we heal ourselves. We also heal our ancestors, our grandmothers, our grandfathers, and our children. When we heal ourselves, we also heal our Mother Earth, and we heal future generations."

When we transform from caterpillar to butterfly, we will become our true luminous selves and evolve into a higher level in the Cosmos.

Grandmother Julieta of Mexico believes in the power of prayer. "I live in the place of power of prayer. What I see is that unity is what the world must strive for now. In this unity form, everything comes together again. All our relations come together again in circles of people, who are at peace again within themselves and also patient with the ones who have not arrived at such peace yet. These circles need to be formed everywhere, so that we can become one again on the whole planet, in this visible world and in the invisible world."

Grandmother Flordemayo also believes that it is only by living in the moment that we will save ourselves, because when we are living in the moment we feel more alive, more love and community. "If we pray 100 percent in that moment, we can move the consciousness of humanity," she says. "The period of scattered prayers and scattered wishes has ended. We must pray to the spirit of the heavens and the Earth, the spirit of the sacred waters, the spirit of our Mother Earth. We must pray to the spirit of humanity to acknowledge each other as brother and sister, as nations of people that breathe the same air, as nations of people who are being fed by the spirit of ancestors of the sacred waters. If we do not acknowledge this, we will lose our way. So I pray for the moment, I pray to be totally present without ego, with total passion, with total love to Spirit, because it is the only way."

When the 9/11 attacks happened, Grandmother Flordemayo went into intense prayer and asked the Grandmothers from the Spirit World to give her understanding of the event. In a vision the north wall of her be room seemed to disappear and she was shown angels gathering in a circle. The angels were so big, they might have been ten to eighteen feet tall. They had huge wings that touched the sky and the Earth. In the middle of the circle was a holy man. The angels began singing, in a heaven celestial way.

Grandmother Flordemayo's vision was that when we pray for peace and acknowledge prayer we are in the sacred circle of angels.

From all that I have learned from the indigenous people of North American and the messages given by the thirteen indigenous Grandmothers, the only thing that separates us from each other is our prejudices and hate. When we learn that we need to come from pure heart as One, and stop destroying our natural resources, killing each other and abusing the creatures of the planet, and when we see everything on Earth as sacred, then spiritual doors of ancient knowledge will become available to us. Our planet will be transformed.

It is this disrespect and greed that has brought us to this dire place in Earth's history. And this disrespect is spreading into us in the form of cancers and many illnesses because we are out of balance—*ayni*.

Children are born into the world full of pollution while in the womb from the toxins in their mother's system, Grandmother Flordemayo explains. The first breast milk an infant receives is tainted with the chemicals the mother carries in her body from the creams, shampoos, hair dyes and cosmetics she uses, not to mention the toxins in our food, the GMOs, and plastics we absorb daily.

Is it any wonder we are seeing a greater number of young children and young adults dying of cancers? While growing up in Idaho during the 1950s and 1960s I don't recall anyone ever having cancer in my schools, but now I read about children everywhere dying of cancer at such young ages, and it greatly saddens me that our new children are leaving the Earth so soon. We need these souls desperately to heal our planet and bring in the higher vibrational rate. At times, I feel this is being orchestrated by dark forces to stop the spiritual evolution of the new children coming into the Earth now.

I had a dream recently where I was shown two Earths in the sky and told that Star Beings are creating a new world where clean air, clean water, animals and plants thrive and humans live in peace. Although the dream was a utopian dream, and the thought is truly wonderful, I believe we need to take care of business here and now, and not dream of new worlds created by extraterrestrials. In other words, we have to clean up our own mess and create a new world.

We all possess great energy within our bodies and in our hands. There are individuals and children who are able to hold their hands together and make a piece of paper ignite. Those with this increased energy will find they can use it to purify food, heal, clean the oceans, and depollute the rivers and lands. Toxic pollution that is everywhere will be transmuted and changed by these beings and new children in the near future. As people gather in groups they will discover that with practice they can work miracles with their gifts as a collective. This gift will apply to healing.

The Earth has been warning us lately, according to the Grandmothers. And now we need to listen as Earth changes accelerate and manifest in destructive hurricanes, typhoons, powerful tornadoes never seen before, torrential rains and floods, devastating earthquakes, as Mother Earth prepares herself for balance again. It is humanity's wake up call to the destruction we caused her and our disrespect for all Mother Earth's creation.

Black Elk was an Oglala Lakota holy man born in 1863 and who died in 1950. When Black Elk was a young boy he had a

Earth Energy

powerful vision from the spirit world after becoming ill. In the vision two men descended with flaming spears. They took him up on a cloud to a great plain. There a bay horse greeted him, accompanied by horses of different colors: black, white, sorrel (red) and buckskin (gold) or the four directions. Leaving the horse, Black Elk traveled to the rainbow-covered lodge, the lodge of the Six Grandfathers (the power of the four quarters, or four directions) of the universe and of Mother Earth and Father Sky.

The first Grandfather represented the power of the West and gave Black Elk a cup of water. The second Grandfather was the power of the north and gave him a white wing and sacred herb of sage. The herb provided truth and honesty, strong, healing sustenance for our bodies, Mother Earth, even world governments and leadership. The third Grandfather represented the power of the red dawn rising in the East and gave Black Elk the sacred pipe, the power of peace. The fourth Grandfather, the power of the South, presented Black Elk with a bright red stick sprouting leaves. The tree would grow in the center of the nation. The fifth Grandfather, the spirit of the sky, became an eagle. He spoke, saying that all things of the sky—the winged, the winds, and the stars, would be as relatives and would come to Black Elk and help him. The sixth Grandfather was really Mother Earth, the Earth Spirit. The Earth Spirit took Black Elk outside the lodge and told him the Earth Power would be with him.

In time, the two-leggeds would desperately need Mother Earth's help. Black Elk was told to set the red stick in the center of the yellow hoop and there the tree would grow, and around it people would gather. In time the tree would bloom.

Black Elk was given the vision of Earth becoming sick. The animals, the winged ones, and the four-legged ones grew frightened. All living things became gaunt and sickly. The air and the waters dirtied and smelled foul. Below, Black Elk saw a blue man making the sickness. (Some interpret the Blue Man to be those who pollute the Earth—industry, corporations and government). The powers of the four directions, represented by four horses, charged the Blue Man, but were beaten back. The Grandfathers called upon Black Elk who picked up his bow that transformed into a spear, and he swooped down on the Blue Man, killing him. When the Blue Man fell, all life came back upon the

Earth; all things became healthy again.

Whenever humans have tampered with Mother Nature, something always goes disastrously askew. We still haven't learned that some things in our world should be left alone, whatever that course may be. Perhaps on some strange level the Universe or God consciousness knows what it is doing.

Psychologist and medical anthropologist, Dr. Alberto Villoldo, studied the healing practices of the Amazon and the Andes for more than 25 years. He discovered the Laika people of the Amazon believe we can change just about anything we want in our world, as long as we're willing to take on the karma.

When we as humans let our ego rule and insist that you must control events, you end up in a constant struggle against the universe. Villoldo suggested that it is difficult for us in the Western world to trust that we can achieve peace and happiness if we're not doing something active to bring it about, but embodying peace and happiness does bring it about. Our egos don't want us to believe that we can have infinite power by immersing ourselves in the wisdom of the universe, but it's true.

He gave an example: "Many young people are fascinated by witchcraft because they think it might give them a chance to have great power and control their lives and those around them. They want to believe that a spell will stop a bully from picking on them by casting a spell on them without any consequences. They don't realize the spells, herbs, chanting won't change their lives—only shifting their perception and embodying confidence and grace will change their lives. The Laika don't have to wear special clothing to know they have power and position. When they enter a home, food appears without their having to ask for it, and blessings are bestowed without having been requested. Their presence has a radiance that others respond to, and words or symbols of power are unnecessary."

In Barbara Marciniak's channeled book, *Bringers of the Dawn*, the Pleiadians said, "When human beings make quality of life the number one priority in their lives by honoring the quality of Earth's life, there will be very few Earth changes upon this planet. However, most humans, particularly in the Western world, are concerned with a very different quality of life: how many electronic devices they own, how many clothes are in their closets, and how many cars are in their garages.

"If human beings do not change—if they do not make the shift in values and realize that without Earth they could not be here—then Earth, in its love for its own initiation and its reaching for a higher frequency, will bring about a cleansing that will balance it once again. There is the potential for many people to leave the planet in an afternoon. Maybe then everyone else will begin to wake up to what is going on. There have been events all along stimulating you, encouraging you, and bringing you to the realization that there must be global change. There are grass-roots movements that are going to grow phenomenally. What happens to Earth depends on how willing everyone is to change.

"What is your responsibility in this? How willing are you to change? The time has come not to just talk about it but to *do it*. As you commit to change in your own life, you automatically make the change available to the entire planet.

"Earth is striving for its integrity. The planet feels at this time deprived of its integrity, dishonored, and unloved. Earth loves you and gives you a place to operate; it is a living organism. Earth is about to reestablish its integrity and let you understand the importance of loving yourself by loving Earth. Love yourself and love Earth, because they are the same."

I foresee Earth changes could play an important role in breaking down the old system that no longer works. Earth changes will bring about the collapse of insurance companies, and start a domino effect for large corporations and banks. Earth changes will also bring about compassion for those who suffer during these changes. The human spirit will triumph as men and women go out of their way to help victims of disasters. There will even be heroes. People will bond with one another.

The Pleiadians went on to say, "There are technologies that could clean this place up very quickly if that were the plan. However, as the species at present does not take responsibility for Earth, there would be no point. The present species must learn to honor its nest. All of you must learn to honor your bodies because without your bodies you would not be here, and without Earth, you would not be here. Your body and your planet are your two greatest gifts and the most valuable things you owe. Ideally, you would express a sacredness and honoring and cherishing and love of Earth and your physical being. This would resonate in your home, your property, the land you are associated with, and the land of your body as well.

Native American Prayer
Oh Great Spirit
Who art everywhere
Mystery is thy name

I appreciate your allowance
That I live
And all mystery
which is put before me

Let me always seek knowledge
For you are the source of all knowledge
Help me to avoid ignorance
For it moves me away from thee

I seek to care for the home
This Earth you have provided
Let my thoughts, actions and deeds
Lead me to you
And the Spirit World which waits beyond.

Ed McGaa "Eagle Man" said, "Hopefully, you now have an understanding that we are a part of the whole universe, especially this planet. *Mitakuye Oyasin.* We are related to all things.

Prayers for Mother Earth
Take a few minutes each day to sit down on Mother Earth and tell her you love and honor her. Give an offering of corn meal (organic) or bird seed. Speak to her like you'd talk you're your own mother. Visualize her healthy, alive and vibrant. Visualize oceans teeming with life again, free of pollutants and trash.

Visualize the rivers and lakes running clear again, see the animals, birds, finned ones and insects returning as they once did hundreds of years ago.

Energy Exercise

This exercise can be practiced alone or with other spiritually-minded people. Find a place where you can meditate away from phones and white noise. If you can escape to a river, mountain, lake or ocean, you'll find the energy much greater there (charged with positive ions). Draw a circle or create one with pebbles or stones. Step inside, relax, and still your body, while you visualize a pillar of light coming down from the heavens and filling your head.

Although you can sit on the ground, Corbin Harney suggested that people stand up to pray, with the soles of their feet right next to Mother Earth. If you can take off your shoes, all the better to connect to Earth energy. As Corbin saw it, all living things stand up, upwards. Energy can them come from the bottom of your feet.

Feel the pillar of light pulsating through your cells and your very essence.

Bring the light through each of your chakra points: the Crown Chakra located at the top of the head, the Third Eye located on the forehead between the eyes, the Throat Chakra, the Heart Charka located at the center of the chest above the heart, the Solar Plexus located in the upper part of the stomach, the Sacral Chakra located at the lower part of the abdomen, and the Root Chakra at the tailbone.

Allow the energy of light to enter the ground and into Earth Mother and visualize that pillar of pure white light traveling through Earth and around the planet, in the oceans, the land, the mountains, the rivers, the lakes and the people in those lands. See the light encompassing all creatures big and small.

Now speak to Mother Earth and tell her how much you love her. Tell her that you have come in a sacred way, and then give an offering of corn meal or bird seed. Organic tobacco can be used. You can also burn sage or sweetgrass during your ceremony. Some prefer to chant or sing. Om or Oh is a great way to chant.

If you have a rock or crystal you want to return to Mother Earth, this is a great way to show your reverence. It is a symbol of the value you have inside yourself and your gift to Earth. As you energize the planet, feel the pillar of light energizing you. Ask how you can make a difference for Earth now.

Pray for the four directions, pray for truth, pray for healing, pray for knowledge, pray for everlasting love, pray for forgiveness and compassion.

Web of Life Prayer by Chief Seattle
Teach your children what we have taught our children - that the Earth is our Mother. Whatever befalls the Earth befalls the sons and daughters of the Earth. If men spit upon the ground, they spit upon themselves. This we know. The Earth does not belong to us, we belong to the Earth. This we know. All things are connected like the blood that unites one family. All things are connected. Whatever befalls the Earth befalls the sons and daughters of the Earth. We did not weave the web of life; we are merely a strand in it. Whatever we do to the Web, We do to ourselves.

Earth Prayer by Black Elk
Grandfather, Great Spirit, once more behold me on Earth and lean to hear my feeble voice. You lived first, and you are older than all need, older than all prayer. All things belong to you—the two-legged, the four-legged, the wings of the air, and all green things that live. You have set the powers of the four quarters of the Earth to cross each other. You have made me cross the good road and road of difficulties, and where they cross, the place is holy. Day in, day out, forevermore, you are the life of things. Hey! Lean to hear my feeble voice.

At the center of the sacred hoop you have said that I should make the tree to bloom. With tears running, O Great Spirit, my Grandfather, with running eyes I must say the tree has never bloomed. Here I stand, and the tree is withered. Again, I recall the great vision you gave me. It may be that some little root of the sacred tree still lives. Nourish it then that it may leaf and bloom and fill with singing birds! Hear me, that the people may once again find the good road and the shielding tree.

Black Elk had many visions of the future and according to his cousin Benjamin, he was in the sweat lodge when a circular craft came out of the sky and hovered over it. Suddenly a stone penetrated the closed door and landed between Black Elk's feet. He picked up the stone but had to complete the sweat lodge ceremony before he could leave. By the time he was able to leave the lodge the spacecraft was gone. Black Elk carried the stone with him the rest of his life with his vision of bringing together all people of the four directions--Red, White, Black and Yellow.

Earth Healing Ceremony by Medicine Grizzly Bear – Spokane, Washington 1990

O Great Creator, I come before you in a humble manner and offer you this sacred pipe. With tears in my eyes and an ancient song from my heart I pray. To the four powers of Creation, To the Grandfather Sun, To the Grandmother Moon, To the Mother Earth, And to my ancestors. I pray for my relations in Nature, All those who walk, crawl, fly, and swim, Seen and unseen, To the good spirits that exist in every part of Creation. I ask that you bless our elders and children, families, and friends, and the brothers and sisters who are in prison. I pray for the ones who are sick on drugs and alcohol and for those who are now homeless and forlorn. I also pray for peace among the four races of humankind.

May there be good health and healing for this Earth, May there be Beauty above me, May there be Beauty below me, May there be Beauty in me, May there be Beauty all around me. I ask that this world be filled with Peace, Love, and Beauty.

Universal Meditation

This is the meditation for three people. Remove your shoes to feel Earth energy. Draw a circle and within the circle, draw a hexagon (six-sided hexagon shown below), and step inside leaving a gap between each person.

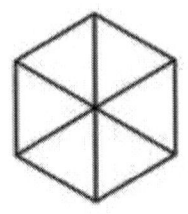

Standing inside the circle, stretch out your hands, arms and touch the person's palm next to you, so you are touching each other's hands with your fingers pointed upward. You have formed a triangle. Bow your head in reverence and begin to chant Om or Oh for several minutes! Clear your minds as you receive the universal energy—it's powerful!

I've been told that neophytes trying this meditation exercise experience beams of light within the circle and around their heads. You may need to stop the exercise within minutes due to the increase in energy. As you continue this exercise, you'll build to 10 minutes. If you attempt this meditation, I suggest you allow only serious-minded people who want to create an energy ring for only the highest good. You can create a circle of six, but make sure that you connect palm to palm, with fingertips pointed upward, and then experience the energy.

You say ecology. We think the words Mother Earth have a deeper meaning. If you wish to survive, we must respect her. It is very late, but there is still time to revive and discover the old American Indian value of respect for Mother Earth. She is very beautiful, and already she is showing us signs that she may punish us for not respecting her. Also, we must remember she has been placed in this universe by the one who is the All Powerful, the Great Spirit Above, or Wakan Tanka—God. —Ed McGaa "Eagle Man"

Epilogue

My wish is that everyone reading this book will reconnect to Mother Earth and Earth Wisdom like the Ancient Ones and indigenous people throughout the world. The Lakota Sioux have a saying, *Mitakuye Oyasin*, which means, *we are related to all things*. Here's the amazing part about the saying—it's true! All living organisms store genetic information using the same molecules—DNA and RNA. Written in the genetic code of these molecules is compelling evidence of the shared ancestry with all living things.

    I know that everything has a consciousness, even rocks, and everything evolves toward the God Source. Plants, trees, and flowers have a living source, which ancient humans understood. It is only in our modern world that such Ancient Wisdom has been forgotten.

    As Earthkeepers practicing Earth Wisdom we can start by

seeing the moment as perfect and then we can change anything we want. The Inca Wisdomkeepers say that once we step outside of time into infinity, the past and future disclose themselves to us—everything becomes clear. Psychic Edgar Cayce said that 12 billion years ago, the energy gestalt we call God, existed in an unmanifested void, and so it decided to experience itself, and produced the big bang, forming all matter in our universe and other universes. God continued to explore itself through all forms of matter—worlds, planets, stars, animals, insects, rocks, water and all beings. It was both omnipresent and omniscient, and so were all its manifestations. If such a scenario is true, how can we deny our power and our connection to the Creator of all things?

As my friend, Corbin Harney taught, "As we all know, our water is going to be pretty precious. I think we all realize this today. I talk about this, and I hope people out there will continue to talk about this, and not be behind the bush like I was. I used to be behind the bush with what I know; I never could come out from behind the bush. Now it's time for us all to come out from behind the bush and start hollering. I don't care how we do it, as long as we do it together."

Like Corbin, I used to be behind the bush, afraid to speak my mind and tell people of the things I've been shown in visions and dreams through the years. No one was listening years ago. Now it's time for everyone to be courageous and step forward as Earthkeepers and Lightkeepers about the abuse of our planet and the changes taking place. If we don't use our voices, all will be lost.

Shortly after my seventh birthday I was shown vivid dreams of cataclysmic Earth changes—tsunami waves hitting coastal shores, volcanoes erupting, earthquakes shaking the land and ferocious winds. Since that time I've been warned of earthquakes, solar flares and even volcanic eruptions. I'm not sure where these visions come from—spirit guides, my guardian angels or interdimensional beings, but I do know it's true and real and I must trust the information. My visions are taking place at this time, and my sense is that something momentous is about to happen to our world.

In Dr. Ardy Sixkiller Clarke's book, *Sky People,* she

interviewed Maya elders and indigenous people of Belize and Guatemala, and many of them said the Sky People warned them of a time of great change. They have been told that there will be wars and Earth shaking, that we are living in the fourth world, but a fifth world is coming, and now it's too late to stop it. They have been told that many sad things are about to happen to Earth. There will be signs in the heavens if people will take the time to look skyward, but the elders say people are too busy to look.

On Maya elder told her that, "This is the fourth world, Señora. It has been destroyed before. Each time, people were careless with the Earth. There is a reason why we are here. We were placed on this planet to look after it. We have been allowed to evolve as a people [the Maya], but we have not been able to perform the task given to us. A day is coming when we must answer for our disregard of our mission. On that day, the Earth will be turned upside down. They [the Sky people] warn us that we must prepare for the future."

In a June 18, 2012 BBC documentary on Nibiru, elders of an indigenous tribe in a remote area of Alaska stated that they have observed strange things in the sky. The sun no longer sets behind a certain mountain as it has for years and the stars are not in the right position as they have observed for decades. They ask if the Earth has tilted on its axis or changed its tilt. These are people who have spent their entire lives outdoors each day and have noted the strange things happening to the sun and the stars.

If the indigenous people have observed these major changes with the setting sun and the position of the stars, then our governments know something drastic has happened to Earth, and they aren't talking.

These changes don't surprise me because I have expected them for many decades and watched the signs in the heavens and on Earth—UFO, orbs, mysterious booms heard world, giant cracks forming in Africa, Russia and in California, sea creatures and birds dying, and other anomalies. I know there will be other signs as Earth changes escalate in the coming years with extreme weather, the moon, stars and sun not in their normal positions, earthquakes in places not known for earthquake activity, sink holes forming, increased volcanic activity and strange lights in the sky.

When humans return to Earth mindfulness and hold our planet

and all living creatures in the highest reverence, then we have taken the next step in our spiritual evolution. We will discover ways to live in harmony with our environment instead of destroying it and then Mother Earth will respond in kind—our thoughts and actions are reflected in her.

It's no coincidence that film director James Cameron's epic 2009 movie, *Avatar,* became a mega hit. The movie focused on a powerful environmental message that the senseless expansion and destruction of our environment has a butterfly effect. It affects all life on Earth. What the movie conveyed to audiences was it's time for humanity to open our eyes and hearts and see the world around us, the network of energy that flows through all living things on Mother Earth.

It's time to say we've had enough of this insanity and disrespect for our Mother Earth. It's time to practice and live *ayni,* and not only the Earth, but the universe will respond in kind to our actions. Time to walk in balance on the Earth and revere all things as divine, and created by Great Spirit or God. When we awaken to the unseen world, the spirit elements, and beings that surround our world and interact with us daily, we will have reached a perfect place of peace, grace and understanding. But we will need to drop our egos like the purity of animals, and stop thinking that we are superior to all other life. We are equal to all.

Spiritual leader Corbin Harney reminded us, "Always offer something to what you get off the land. Bless what you get off Mother Earth. Bless the water. Talk to it, keep it alive, keep it moving, keep the spirit in the water moving. If you talk to it and bless it, it really keeps the water happy, gives it strength."

We must teach our children a new way of living, in order to ensure future generations will have a beautiful Earth to enjoy and the abundance the Creator has given us. The Grandmothers tell us it is important to teach the children of the world how to humbly pray to the rocks, the trees, the sky, the mountains, the sacred waters, the birds, and all animals. Like the Grandmothers, Ed McGaa and Corbin, I am also deeply concerned about the younger generation and their future. The younger people have become so addicted to technology, their cell phones, video games, texting, they have forgotten the natural world, the real world—it's sad for them and humanity and sad for Mother Earth. Humanity has become lost in technology and the real world—the nature world. How will most of us survive if a great catastrophe should befall our planet? How will the young people survive without Earth Wisdom? That's why we must teach them the knowledge of Earth. Indigenous tribes who continue to practice the natural way will survive because this has been their way of life for eons. They understand the spirit elements and the signs Mother Earth provides. They listen with open hearts—unlike most of us who have closed our hearts and myopic minds.

Corbin believed it is very important to do the ceremonies and prayers. It's very important for all of us to get together again and again to honor Earth. He said, "Some of you go to church and pray together. That is very important, and it's what we must do. We have to pray to the sun, the Earth, the water, and to the air. I hope that we will all pick up this message that I'm putting out, so that we can have a cleaner life, and so the younger generation can continue on."

We are connected to the Great Mystery. Through my own paranormal and spiritual experiences I've learned there is so much more to life than what our normal senses perceive. There are other realities and life forms that coexist with us in other realities. There are ghosts, spirits, angels, fairies, and deities that reside in our world—mostly unseen. Instead of having closed eyes, we need to open our eyes and minds to other possibilities, other realities, and realize that nothing is impossible, and everything is possible.

We are fortunate to have taken on physical bodies to experience life at its fullest, to see with our physical eyes a sunset, a brilliant red sunrise, a rainbow arched across the sky, and an aurora borealis lighting up the night sky in vivid colors. Life is a circle, as the ancients taught, and everything returns to the Oneness of life.

As Earth changes increase, our bodies will feel the vibrational change. There are huge dynamics taking place within and on Mother Earth, and every living thing will be touched by those changes. If we believe the Hopi and that we are in the Purification Times, then the Prophecy Rock tell us that we have a choice. Will we save Mother Earth or watch her perish? Together, united, we can make a difference, and if you don't believe consciousness can affect change through intent and prayer, consider this: two of NOAAs (National Oceanic and Atmospheric Administrations) space weather satellites known as GOES-8 and GOES-10 that monitor Earth's geomagnetic field picked up a huge spike during the September 11, 2001 attack on the World Trade buildings, and several days after the attacks. Many theorized the spike indicated there were stress waves caused by mass human emotion on Earth's geomagnetic field. GOES-8, orbiting 22, 300 miles above the equator that day, detected a surge that topped out at nearly 50 units (nano testlas), higher than any previous recording. The time was 9 a.m. eastern standard time, 15 minutes after the first plane hit the World Trade Center and about minutes before the second impact.

Our thoughts, our fears, our anger, our love, our hate, go directly into Mother Earth. She feels us, and we feel her. If the majority of Earth people are locked in fear, where do you think that negative emotion goes? It's pure energy and it goes into the ether and into Mother Earth.

When we begin to understand the divinity, the cosmology of all life, we will no longer take our beautiful planet for granted, the Grandmothers tell us. They say in these days, when the prophecies are being fulfilled, we are the ones who will determine whether or not we will destroy our Mother Earth and ourselves. Each us have an obligation to decide whether or not to live in harmony and with a selfless love for the benefit of all. Not only do we have an obligation to ourselves but to future generations still unborn.

WHAT WILL OUR LEGACY BE FOR FUTURE GENERATIONS—DESTRUCTION OF MOTHER EARTH OR A WORLD OF BEAUTY AND BALANCE?

The Grandmothers say it is important to create a more personal sense of connection by holding rituals, ceremonies, and festivals. It is then that we speak directly to the spirit elements and Mother Earth. Ritual engages the spirit of a place, a circuit of energy in which the entire cosmos participates. There was a time, the Grandmothers remind us, when all of our ancestors revered Earth and used ceremonies to hold Earth's balance. Today, that balance no longer exists.

"Prayer is the greatest thing I have as I walk upon this Earth," Grandmother Agnes of Oregon says. 'I am nothing without the

Creator. When you have the Creator with you, you have the force behind you, and negativity doesn't take over you, even in the dreamtime. You can't change even your children, except through prayer. Prayer is a duty that has been handed down from the Ancient Ones that went before us."

To be an Earthkeeper start with self- love and radiate that love outward—love Mother Earth, all her creation, and love all humanity. Eagle Man says, "Our survival is dependent on the realization that Mother Earth is a truly holy being, that all things in this world are holy and must not be violated, and that we must share and be generous with one another. Think of your fellow men and women as holy people who were put here by the Great Spirit. Think of being related to all things! With this philosophy in mind as we go on with our environmental ecology efforts, our search for spirituality, and our quest for peace, we will be far more successful when we truly understand the Indians' respect for Mother Earth."

In these times of great change, trust your intuition, trust what the creatures tell you, trust the sky, the ocean, the elements, the insects, the birds, the sea creatures to warn you when Earth starts to move in a big way. Speak to Mother Earth and ask her to guide you to safety areas—she hears your words.

The most astonishing fact is that you are made up of stars, nebulas, galaxies, black holes—the very fabric of the universe. In other words—you are literally STARDUST, the atoms and molecules of the universe. Now it's time to start acting like the remarkable spiritual beings we were created to be by honoring Mother Earth and all life.

Astronomer, cosmologist and astrophysicist Carl Sagan (1934-1996) left us with his beautiful words of wisdom in his book, *The Pale Blue Dot,* "If you look at Earth from space you see a dot, that's here. That's home. That's us! It underscores the responsibility to deal more kindly and compassionately with one another and to preserve and cherish that pale blue dot, the only home we've ever known. Thank you all."

As the Lakota Sioux have always known, *Mitakuye Oyasin— we are all related!*

Living Earth Wisdom by Ed McGaa "Eagle Man and Betsey:

Bring back the natural harmony that humans once enjoyed.

Honor your body, your living temple, with natural food, sleep and exercise.

Love and forgive all. Rid yourself of prejudice.

Practice real truth each day.

Take time each day to pray, visualize, meditate, intend a new world, a healed planet for all.

Gratitude: appreciate your life, the planet and all blessings that come into your life.

Practice ceremony—the indigenous way or your own way. Take time to practice reverence. Take time to hug a tree, smell flowers, and give thanks to all life. Remove your shoes and talk to Mother Earth. Listen to the frogs and crickets toning and anchoring Earth's grid. Find moving water, and feel the negative ions. Feel the elemental spirits.

Be kind to animals, and give thanks to the animals you eat!

Honor and cherish children.

Teach your children Earth Wisdom, and how to honor life.

Disconnect as much as possible from negative news, cell phones, computers, television and electronics. Reconnect with Mother Earth.

Be brave and courageous enough to take a stand and make a commitment. Let your voice be heard.

Share with others and be less materialistic.

Be magnanimous of self and charitable to others.

Recycle, recycle, recycle everything! Clean up trash and plastic in city parks and national parks. If you pack it in, pack it out!

Trust your intuition, trust Earth Mother and trust the creatures to warn you when the planet begins to move.

Laugh and love more. Practice compassion.

Find solitude in natural sounds of nature and soothing music that heals. Music is a healing vibration.

Be kind to yourself as the powerful spiritual being you are.

Bibliography

Benveniste, Jacques. Article in *Nature* magazine 1988.

Breytenbach, Anna. Award-winning documentary, *The Animal Communicator* (Dec. 2013)

Cheney, Margaret. *Man Out of Time* (New York, NY: Touchstone 1981 and 2001).

Clarke, Ardy Sixkiller. *Sky People* (Pompton Plains, NJ: New Page Book 2015).

Collins, Andrew. *The Cygnus Mystery* (London, UK: Watkins Publishing 1999)

Emoto, Masaru Dr. *Message from Water: The Hidden Messages in Water* (Hillsboro, OR: Beyond Words Publishing 2004).

Chasse, Betsey, Artntz, William and Vicente, Mark. *What the Bleep Do we Know: Down the Rabbit Hole* (Documentary 2005).

Harney, Corbin. *The Way It Is* (Nevada City, NV: Blue Dolphin Publishing, Inc. 1995).

Hill, Julia Butterfly. *The Legacy of Luna* (San Francisco, CO: Harper san Francisco 2001

LaChapelle, Dolores. *Earth Wisdom* (Los Angeles, CA: The Guild of Tutors Press 1978).

Linn, Denise. *Sacred Space* (New York, NY: Random House 1995).

Marciniak, Barbara. *Earth, Bringers of the Dawn and Family of Light* (Santa Fe, NM: Bear & Co., Inc. 1992 -1999).

McClean, Dorothy. *Seeds of Inspiration* (The Lorian Association

2004).

McCorkell, Don. *A River of Waste: The Hazardous Truth about Factory Farms* (Documentary 2008).

McFadden, Steven. *Ancient Voices: The Legend of the Rainbow Warriors* (Santa Fe, NM: Bear and Co., Inc. 1992).

McGaa, Ed. *Mother Earth Spirituality (*New York, NY: HarperSan Franciso 1990), *Rainbow Tribe (*New York, NY: HarperSanFrancisco 1992) *Spirituality for America, Creator's Code.*

O'Barry, Ric. (Academy award-winning documentary, *The Cove* 2009).

Phan-Le, Marie Rose. *Talking Story* (Berkeley, CA: North Atlantic Books 2014).

Pratt, Heather, MNT. Natural Grocers Magazine May 2014 issue Roberts, Jane. *Seth Speaks* (San Rafael, CA: Amber-Allen Publishing 1972 and 1999).

Sagan, Carl. *A Pale Blue Dot* (New York, New York: Ballantine Books 1997)

Sanderson, Ivan. T. *Invisible Residents* (Kempton, Illinois: Adventures Unlimited Reprint 2007)

Schaeffer, Carol. *Grandmothers Counsel the World* (Boston, MA: Trumpeter Books 2006).

Sitchin, Zecharia. *The 12th Planet* (Rochester, Vermont: Bear & Co. 1976, 1978, 1991).

Soll, David. *Empire Water* (Ithaca, NY: Cornell University Press 2013).

Sun Bear and Wabun. *The Medicine Wheel: Earth Astrology*

(Englewood Cliffs, New Jersey: Prentice-Hall 1980).

Tsarion, Michael. *Atlantis:Alien Visitation and Genetic Manipulation* (Seattle, WA: Unslaved Media 2011).

Villoldo, Alberto Ph.D. *The Four Insights* (Carlsbad, CA: Hay House, Inc. 2006).

Watkins, Alfred. *The Old Straight Track,* first published in 1925. (Abacus Publisher 1988).

Wetherford, Jack. *Genghis Khan and the Making of the Modern World* (New York, NY: Crown Publishers 2004).

Woodward, Heather. *Ghosts of Central Arizona* (Pennsylvania: Schiffer Publishing 2010).

About the Author

Betsey Lewis is a renowned psychic, the host of Rainbow Vision Network, an Earth mysteries investigator, and Earthkeeper. Beginning at age three, the paranormal has been the normal for her with two UFO encounters and communication with the Other Side. Betsey has investigated and researched UFO sightings, cattle mutilations, angels, aliens, and other earth mysteries for over forty years. She lives the medicine way of life taught to her by indigenous leaders Corbin Harney and Ed McGaa "Eagle Man." She practices Reiki, Kriya Yoga, numerology, astrology, and regressive hypnosis.

Betsey has appeared on Idaho's KTVB noon show, KIVI morning show, The Dr. Michael TV Show, and has been a guest on many well-known radio shows including Coast-to-Coast AM with George Noory, KTAK's The Fringe, Fade to Black with Jimmy Church and Ground Zero. She was also a featured keynote speaker at the 2012 Alamo UFO Conference near Las Vegas, Nevada.

Published books include: *Communicating with The Other Side—True Experiences of a Psychic-Medium, Never Can Say Goodbye, Mystic Revelations of Thirteen, Angels, Aliens and Prophecy II,* and three children's stories—*Alexander Phoenix, A Worm Named Sherm* and *The Story of Rainbow Eyes.* Coming soon: *Super Kids—The New Evolved Kids Have Arrived.* For more information on Betsey's psychic practice, her articles, her books, her radio show, scheduling workshops/speaking engagements, and her daily Earth News1 blog, visit: betseylewis.com.

Made in the USA
San Bernardino, CA
07 October 2016